To

Kerry

The Wizard of Was

Soooooon!

Love

Matt xx

The Wizard of Was

A Practical Guide to Eliminating
Self Sabotage

Matt Hudson

authorHOUSE®

AuthorHouse™
1663 Liberty Drive
Bloomington, IN 47403
www.authorhouse.com
Phone: 1-800-839-8640

Published by AuthorHouse   04/28/2012

ISBN: 978-1-4567-8634-2 (sc)
ISBN: 978-1-4567-8635-9 (e)

Contents

WARNING: This book contains extremely powerful techniques which have the ability to help people change their thought patterns and should therefore be used with due attention and consideration.

"Words are, of course, the most powerful drug used by mankind."
Rudyard Kipling.

"Truth is incontrovertible; malice may attack it and ignorance may deride it; but, in the end; there it is."
Winston Churchill

Let me tell you a little story . . .

Looking Forward to Chapter One.

"Be Free of your Past, Create your Future."
Tad James.

"The link between all of our memories, our experiences, emotions, expectations and aspirations provides us with both foundation and direction. When you know where those memories are, when you know where to best position your future desires, then you have discovered a very powerful tool indeed to help you in life."

The human mind is elusive and infinite.

- Elusive because here we are in the 21st Century and still science can not find where the mind resides.
- Infinite because we have centuries of evidence to support how wonderful the mind is and how creative it can be.

  The co nnection between what we experience as individuals within this life can only be represented in metaphor as each of us experiences the world differently. For this reason we have chosen to give you the information within a story, thus allowing your mind to wield your own magic!

The book is designed to support you in letting go of yesterday's problems. Satir said "the problem isn't the problem, coping is" so we aim to give you more tools to help you to cope.

If you were to stop and think about your life for a moment and really think about yourself right now, you are breathing and that's okay. The challenge for most people is when they bring yesterday with them on an unconscious level. They continue to struggle with the pains, torments, arguments and guilt from many years earlier, it is here that I realised, if you gave yourself permission to take the learning out of yesterday then you could move forward with an unlimited amount of choices and, to that end, I hope that you can leave your troubles in Was.

Chapter One

Into the World of Was

I believe that man will not merely endure, he will prevail.
He is immortal, not because he alone among the creatures
has an inexhaustible voice, but because he has a soul, a
spirit capable of kindness and compassion.

William Faulkner.

"Only some of them do." The elf grumpily dumped the dishes in the self-washing sink and turned to face the Wizard.

"They *all* do, Elf. Or at least they all can if they want to . . . That's what makes it all so interesting." The Wizard smiled down at his helper, and winked.

"Hmmph," said the elf named Elf. He turned away from his master and scuttled on short, dumpy legs across the flagstone floor towards a round oak door.

"No really, Elf. That's the wonder of it." The Wizard's smile got even wider as he followed the elf out of the kitchen. "Just imagine, it's a technique that everyone can use to turn time to their advantage. To get an insight into hindsight."

"Well, we don't exactly get thousands of them queuing up to become enlightened—if anything, interest in us has seemed to slow down recently." The elf risked a grin of his own but kept a wary eye on his boss. Working for Wizards—even good Wizards—was a notoriously risky business, and life as a magical minion was challenging enough without the added indignity of getting turned into a toad.

"You know, for once, you've got a point there. Let us hope that the helping people business speeds up!" The Wizard came to a stop in the long tower corridor, followed a few second later by his purple robes which settled around him, making a swishing sound.

"I have a point? That's not like me!" The elf stood, eyebrows raised in exasperation.

"Yes, I'll admit it's unusual, but valid non-the-less. A lot of people don't know, don't care, or are oblivious about how to help themselves." Said the Wizard, who was now concentrating on a thick black velvet curtain covering the corridor's window. He twitched the curtain aside, affording the elf a brief glimpse of purple sky and swirling clouds.

"Oh, Thanks." Elf said, half annoyed at being ignored yet again, half relieved that the Wizard was too caught up in his musings to notice how sarcastic he was being.

"Don't mention it," the Wizard smiled, "What we need, Elf, is better publicity. A means of making the technique known to people without having to wait for them to find us."

"Maybe you can take over their talking lanterns, Computevision 's the name I think? The elf looked up at the Wizard, wondering if this was going to be one of those oh-so-rare occasions when he was praised for coming up with two good ideas in a row.

"Mess with man-magic?" The Wizard shot his assistant a look of incredulity. "No. I know nothing of . . . of elastic trickery, or whatever it is they call it." The Wizard walked as he talked, heading with unerring ease along the tower's twisting, ever changing passageways.

"Pardon me, oh wise one." The elf muttered, little legs pumping hard to keep up with the Wizard's retreating robes.

"Naturally, Elf. Don't I pardon you dozens of times a day; forgiving your many mistakes and moribund misgivings?" He raised a hand, twirling it expansively without looking back at the now glowering elf.

"Indeed, sir, you certainly spend a great deal of time correcting my every word. So, if not Computevision, how *are* we going to spread the word? Do you intend to run seminars? Put out pamphlets? Take out an ad in 'Wizard's Weekly?'"

"Come with me, and you shall see!" The Wizard said cryptically, keeping up his brisk robe swishing pace. They had reached the spacious central hall and the Wizard was heading purposefully for the spiral stone staircase that wound upwards to the Tower's tapered top. Feet hidden under his robes, the magician seemed to glide effortlessly up the stairs followed at a slower pace by his not so graceful companion, who viewed the large stone stairs with all the apprehension of a novice climber confronting a steep cliff face.

"Do try and keep up!" the Wizard's voice drifted back down the stairs.

The elf held his tongue, resisted the urge to comment and instead concentrated on his breathing as he carefully clambered up each steep step, wondering to himself why his barmy boss refused to use the perfectly good tower lift.

"Ah, there you are!" the Wizard grinned at the red faced elf, who was just hauling himself onto the stone floor of the lower landing. The Wiz set off briskly with the little elf in tow.

"Where are we going?" Elf wheezed.

"To the writing room, of course! That's how we wizards have always shared our magic—in magic books. You know that." The Wizard had stopped at a door about halfway down the landing, fingers grasping the handle.

"Oh no. No way." Elf had come to a stop and was waving his small hands, palms outwards, at the Wizard.

"What now. Elf?" the surprise in the Wizard's voice was quickly replaced by realisation. "Oh! You're not still annoyed about the last time you were in here are you? Really. That was just a silly misunderstanding."

"Misunderstanding!" squeaked the elf, "It stabbed me! I've still got the scar!" He rolled up one miniature green trouser leg to reveal a tiny read semicircle-shaped scar on his calf.

"Well, you started it, gnawing away on its top like you did."

"How was I supposed to know the stupid pen was alive?"

"You live in a Wizard's tower, Elf. It shouldn't have come as such a surprise. Anyway, enough of your whingeing. We've got work to do, remember, and the pen is going to help us—in fact, it already is." The Wizard of Was swung open the writing room door, revealing a small candle-lit space dominated by a circular oak table on which lay a large leather-bound book opened to near its beginning. Above it there hovered an old-fashioned looking fountain pen—the type that normally needs dipping in an inkwell every few lines. Elf let out a strangled squawk and ran behind the Wizard's robes.

"Don't be such a wimp." Laughed the Wizard, shaming Elf just enough for him to peer cautiously around his master's robes. The pen had stopped hovering and started moving steadily across the empty vellum page; making soft scratching noises and writing 'The Wizard of Was' as it went.

Elf watched the pen suspiciously, "Well, I still don't trust it. It might be writing now, but it can move as fast as a diving bird and that nib is so *sharp*, and I can't remember who told me—I think it was some writer—but whoever it was said that 'the pen is mightier than the sword,' and I believe them."

"Oh, really? You are so suspicious, Elf. The pen is being perfectly peaceful, scribbling away, and who ever heard of believing a writer? Everyone knows that they are always making things up!"

"Well I still say that the thing is dangerous." Elf tutted.

"And I," the Wizard let the door swing shut leaving the magic pen to its task, "still say that you are one very wimpy elf!" They retraced their steps across the lower landing; Elf was torn between feelings of relief at being away from the writing room and dread at approaching the mountainous stairs.

"But that," continued the Wizard of Was, "is beside the point. The main thing is that once the pen is finished—once it has the Time Technique down on paper—we will be able to reach, to help, so many more people. Maybe one day, we will even be able to reach them all!"

Elf peered up at the dreamy expression on his master's face. "Hmmph! Now we're back to square one, wherever that may be."

"Ay?" The Wizard returned from his reverie. "Back to where Elf?"

"Back to what we were talking about down in the kitchens. With the greatest of respect your Wizardfullness; I still say that, even mentally speaking, they aren't *all* capable of turning time to their advantage. Some, the majority of them probably, aren't even aware of the River of Time and—even amongst those who are conscious of it—most just drift along with the current, trying to avoid the rapids, praying that they don't come to a waterfall, and wistfully remembering the slow flowing shallows of their pasts.

"Eloquently put my little friend," the Wizard had stopped walking to give his short statured assistant the chance of catching up. "You may even be right, but as you say, it *is* possible to turn time to your advantage; and that is what we are going to do with this book. Teach people how. Let them into the secret of the Stepping Stones so that they can skip across the river!"

"I never said that getting knowledge of the Time Technique out there wouldn't help more of them, but I still don't think that it can help *everyone*." Elf began walking again, pumping his little legs fast in the naïve hope of gaining the last word in his discussion with the Wizard; yet he barely made it back to the stairs before the Wizard had glided effortlessly past him.

"Oh, yes it can Elf. It can help every single one—all six billion if they knew about it." The Wizard was smiling his knowing smile again.

"Yes, Wizard." Elf knew when he was beaten, or, more accurately, he had made the judicious decision to stop disagreeing with the Wizard before he got to the pantomime stage of 'Oh yes it is!', 'Oh no it isn't!" which had the risk of annoying his boss, which in turn would lead to him spending many a happy hour doing something really fun that the Wizard had dreamt up, like cauldron polishing.

The Wizard, though, was wise to Elf's ways. "Don't you go 'Yes, Wizarding' me. If I can't persuade you, how can I convince all of the humans? No, Elf, we are just going to have to find a way to change your mind."

"And will this mind changing involve any form of mundane and pointless tower cleaning?" Elf peered up at the Wizard, his eyes narrowing in suspicion.

"No. I think something far more persuasive is in order."

"You're not going to change me into a toad until I agree, or give me huge clown feet or . . ."

"Why no!" The Wizard exclaimed, "When have I ever inflicted such indignities on your little frame?"

"Well, there was that time at the Wizard moot last year when you 'accidentally' zapped me across the room; the time at the guild of magic's Christmas party when that spell you aimed at the plastic reindeer bounced off that silver serving tray and I ended up with a shiny red nose until Easter, or that mock duel you had with the Whiskey wizard when you . . ."

"Yes, yes, never mind about all of that now, Elf. We have to find a way to resolve our little disagreement. It's imperative that I convert you into a total believer!" The Wizard stroked his beard thoughtfully.

"Bet whatever he comes up with will mean more work for me." Elf murmured to himself.

"What was that?"

"Nothing. That is I . . . I never . . . I don't think that . . ."

"Oh never mind, I heard you anyway. That's it! That is what we shall do!" Once again the Wizard was beaming down at Elf—something his little helper found increasingly alarming.

"What is it? What shall we do?" Elf was secretly dreading the Wizard's answer, sure that his boss had heard the 'more work' part of his mutter and that somehow he was in for extra chores.

"Why wager of course. We shall have ourselves a little bet to decide whether the Time Technique works for everyone or just a select few."

"We shall?" Elf was computing the odds, warily considering the Wizard's proposition with all the caution of a mouse twitching its nose at the cheese in a trap.

"Yes—don't you agree that it is a simply splendid and fun idea? A great way to prove who is right or wrong?" The Wizard looked down at Elf expectantly.

"I suppose that you'd be picking the 'test subjects'?" Elf's natural suspicion was coming to the fore, and he strongly suspected that the Wizard had a trick or two up his rather large sleeves.

"Well in the interests of objectivity, I'd have to insist that the 'test subjects' as you've called them, fulfil the basic criteria of all three known groupings of human, that is to say; man, woman, and child. Other than that though, I'm quite confidant that whoever you choose, and wherever they are, I shall most certainly be able to aid them significantly by using the Time Technique."

The Wizard waved his hands with an odd mixture of humility and confidence.

"I get to pick the people?" Elf stared at the Wizard, still looking for the catch.

"Yes, Elf."

"Why? Why do I?"

They had begun walking again, towards the stairs and the tower's next level, discussing the bet as they went. But this one word from Elf brought the Wizard of Was to a sudden stop. The candlelit corridor darkened around them, simultaneously becoming claustrophobic and cavernous. The Wizard himself, already far larger than the diminutive elf, seemed to grow, to become a huge and powerful presence.

"Elf!" he boomed, "You know better than that. How many long years have we toiled together to help people? And you use *that* word? Must I tell you *again* why it is a bad thing to say?"

"No! Sorry oh great sage, oh mighty user of magic. It just slipped out, I know it's bad and I won't ever . . ."

"Think of the big picture, Elf," the Wizard said, ignoring his protesting underling. "You know how challenging, how confrontational, it can be to ask anyone 'why'. You know it relates to personal beliefs and values."

"Yep, yes I do . . . it's just that."

"For example, and do stop mumbling and pay attention."

"I . . ."

"Elf! Ssh! Now where was I? Ah yes, now if you saw someone behaving strangely which questioning word would you use?"

"I'd ask 'Why are they doing that?'" Elf knew better, of course, but as he was in for the full wizarding lecture on why, he thought he might as well get value for money.

"Ah!" The Wizard refused to take the bait and played along, "But you need first to define the 'that,' and to do so you must ask which question?"

"What." Said Elf dutifully, "I must first ask *what* they are doing."

"Exactly! Now if we consider environment, the question would be?"

"Where."

"And, just to reinforce the notion, Behaviour?"

"What."

"Capability?"

"How."

"And finally, Identity?"

"That would be 'Who,' boss."

"Very good, my little friend." The Wizard beamed; "Now has that sunk in or do you require me to go over it one more time, just to be sure."

Elf looked around, trying to pick the best avenue of escape. He briefly considered, and then hastily dismissed, dashing off in the direction of the writing room. With the still looming Wizard filling the rest of the corridor, he decided that the only wise option would be to return to the original course and resume the cumbersome climbing of the tower stairs. The Wizard of Was watched him go with an amused twinkle in his eye.

"Oh do try and keep up Elf!" said the Wizard, his long legs quickly overtaking the elf and beginning to climb the stairs which led to the towers next level.

"But I set off first!" Elf claimed indignantly.

"Sorry, can't hear you. You're too far behind. Come on, we have to get to the Central Information Room if we are to put this bet into action." The Wizard's voice drifted down the stairs.

"Coming!" puffed Elf, the tips of his little fingers grasping the edge of the next large stair, patches of rosy red appearing incongruously on his pallid green skin. "Did I even agree to this bet?" he wondered as he climbed.

The Central Information Room lies on mid-landing in the tower, a well-shaft sunk into the vast lake of knowledge that is at the Wizard's disposal. Via this conduit, he can summon information on any subject known to man, and beyond that, the arcane knowledge known only to wizarding society. After an age Elf arrived, huffing and puffing, on the ornate Oriental rug covering mid-landing's floor. The climb over, he sat heavily (or, at least, as heavily as a little elf can sit) on the ground; head bowed as his lungs pumped like bellows.

"Ah, there you are Elf." The Wizard was leaning languidly against a nearby wall, slurping with gusto from a delicate looking porcelain cup. "You took so long I thought you must have stopped for a tea break so I conjured myself a cup." He raised his cup and saluted the little figure who sat gasping on the rug.

"I . . . did . . . NOT . . . stop . . . for . . . a tea, or . . . any . . . other . . . type . . . of . . . break!" Elf gulped down air.

"Well, no matter. You're here now, and that's what counts." The Wizard let go of his empty cup which fell towards the rug, completing two lazy revolutions before blinking out of existence with a barely audible 'pop.'

Annoying as the Wizard's tea drinking routine was to Elf, it had at least given him time to catch his breath and he struggled to his feet, preparing to follow the Wizard into the Central Information Room. Mid-landing had only one very large central area, surrounded by a narrow corridor encircling the room and leading from the staircase to the oppositely positioned door. It was down this narrow space that the Wizard and Elf walked.

Soon the two figures, one tall and cloaked, the other short and scampering, came to a set of large oaken double doors upon which the letters C. I. R were inscribed boldly in gold. The Wizard placed one hand on each side of the door, palms pressed flatly to the rich grain of the old wood. He murmured quietly, mouthing words in the secret language of wizards, words so magical that even the pointed ears of the elf by his side heard nothing but the sound of wind rushing through tall grass. Finally, the spell of opening completed, the Wizard stood back and the double doors swung inwards revealing a cavernous space, bigger than even the already large external dimensions of the room suggested. The areas curving walls were lined with innumerable charts, some showing recognisable stellar constellations, many others depicting alien skies, alternate dimensions and symbols that defied decryption.

In the centre of the large circular space, there sat a massive machine the colour of an old copper kettle. In common with the room that bore its name, the machine was cylindrical. Lengths of coiled and brightly coloured wire connected it to a surreally shaped monitor which sat atop the main cylinder. The monitor's screen displayed a darkly glowing scroll of text:

The Five Freedoms

The freedom to see and hear what is here, instead of what should be, was and/or will be.

The freedom to say what one feels instead of what one should.

The freedom to feel what one feels instead of what one should.

The freedom to ask for what one wants instead of waiting for permission.

The freedom to take risks in one's behalf instead of wanting only to be secure.

Virginia Satir

"They," said the Wizard pointing to the screen "are my screen saver wisdoms."

"Screen saver wisdoms?" asked Elf.

"Yes, some of the great rules, taught to us wizards by the Great Seer Satir amongst others. In many ways Elf, they encapsulate the enlightenment that I instil in humans by using my magic. But now, back to our bet!"

"Did we, er, actually make the bet?" Elf said uncertainly, "I thought that we were still going over the terms?"

"Don't be such a pedant, my little helper! We've sorted all of that out." The Wizard looked down at the elf. "I tell you what, I'm so confidant that the Time Technique can help absolutely everyone that I'll not merely let you decide on the people we help, and where they are, I'll even let you choose which order we help them in! There, I can't say fairer than that can I Elf? Remember, it was you who said that I couldn't help everyone."

"Well . . ." the elf stroked his chin.

"Elf!"

"Oh go on then, I'll do it." Elf resigned himself to his part in the bet and took a step forward toward the Central Information Machine before stopping again.

"What now Elf?" said the wizard, becoming impatient to get on with the test.

"How do I select the people and place then?"

"Well ask the machine of course!" Tutted the Wizard, as if talking to something which looked like a combination of kettle

15

and computer was the most normal thing in the world. Elf looked sidelong at his boss (this was the first time that he'd been allowed in the inner sanctum of the Wizard's knowledge centre) and took a hesitant step towards the C.I.M

"Hello?" Elf looked at the copper coloured thing but it was either unaware of his presence or deliberately ignoring him (having had a large amount of experience with wizarding paraphernalia over the years, he suspected that it was the latter).

"It's a Kettleputer, not a person." Said the amused Wizard, "You have to use its keyboard." He pointed out a large, elaborately decorated wooden board situated under the strange machine's screen.

"Ah." Elf walked up to the control panel and examined its keys. He found one that was usefully labelled 'On' and, after a brief glance at the Wizard (who nodded his reassurance) pressed it. The screen showing the sayings of the seer Satir dulled momentarily before being replaced with a blinking cursor.

"Um." said Elf, once again looking at the Wizard for advice.

"Oh, here, I'll do it." The Wizard walked over to the keyboard and accessed the database of humanity, causing the machine to display an exceptionally long list of names. "There you go. Pick."

"Right!" said Elf, watching the list of names blur past. He hesitated for a moment before randomly prodding the keyboard, his small finger happening to connect with the 'w' key. Unfortunately for the wizard's confused helper, the list of names continued to tumble past at an alarmingly indecipherable rate, the only difference being that now, all of the names began with 'w.'

"Stop dithering, Elf."

"There!" Elf pointed at the blurry list of names on the screen, "I want that one!"

"Which one?" The wizard looked at the list and back at Elf.

"Um, that one," mumbled Elf, "they go past so quickly, it's hard to choose . . . Watch!" Elf pointed at the screen of W's.

"Watch what? Ah! The Watch family." Remarked the wizard, "An apt choice, Elf. How very astute—I am impressed."

"Er, yep—them." Elf was just glad that the trauma of choosing was over, and hoped that now he could escape the dreaded kettleputer thing.

"All of them?" The wizard seemed momentarily surprised, "I half expected you to make a more diverse choice, but I suppose that there are three of them: a man, a woman, and a child, so we have all bases covered. Perhaps you are trying to be especially cunning and set me the supposedly difficult challenge of dealing with their familial and interpersonal relationships in order to thoroughly test the Time Technique. Is that it?" The wizard looked at Elf with a rare expression of respect on his face.

"Yes. That's it." Elf hoped that he sounded confident, as he wasn't quite sure what the Wizard was going on about.

"Well. Which one first?" The Wizard pressed a couple of keys and the list of names was replaced by a grouping of three—Timmy, Tania and Tony—under the heading 'Watch.'

"Timmy," said Elf, for no other reason than that it was the first name on the list.

"Right!" replied the wizard, "Young Timmy Watch it is. Follow me. We're going to the Time Room."

The wizard turned, walking towards the door when Elf's voice called him back.

"Wait! The screen's changing."

Basic Timeline Exercise:

Using a blank piece of paper create a chart like the one bellow.

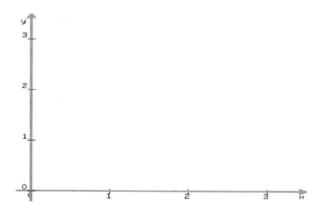

On the Y axis mark it from 0-10) where 10 equals the best.

On the X axis put the number of years you have been alive.

Now plot your happiness from birth to date.

I like nonsense it wakes up the brain cells.
Dr Seuss.

Everything you are against weakens you,
everything you are for empowers you.
Wayne Dyer.

Remember a real decision is measured
by the fact that you've taken new action.
If there's no action, you haven't truly decided.
Anthony Robbins.

Chapter Two

There's a Time to Learn

You can acquire information from reading a book but to experience you must creatively respond to information. Acquiring information is passive. Experience is active.

Maxwell Maltz. *Pyscho-Cybernetics.*

The Wizard of Was looked at the C.I.M screen and saw that Elf was right. The rules of the seer Satir had faded out and been replaced. "Ah yes," he said, "This is the machine being clever. Clever indeed. These are the words of the great Doctor C.D. Larson. We would do well to bear this in mind when we visit young Timmy."

From ***The Scientific Training of Children***:

"*It is the truth and a most important truth that genius does exist in the subconscious of every mind. Every child is born with that interior something which, when developed, can produce remarkable ability, extraordinary talent, and rare genius. It is* therefore of the highest importance that the mind be so trained that all of its latent power and capacity be developed, because everybody should be given the opportunity to reach his potential. I believe the dull child has the talent of the bright child and his mind can be made active. It is only a matter of knowing how. I also believe a dull child is dull due to an improper conditioning of the mind from childhood. Improper conditioning of the mind could mean that the mind was neglected, that his talents died from neglect and full use of the elements were not brought forth, or he was suppressed, frequently punished without reason, constantly told in many ways that he is dumb; thus his energy drained to the point of following primitive tendencies.

I believe to suppress energy is not only to waste energy, it is worse than that, for continued suppression will after a while decrease the amount of energy generated. The less energy one generates in his system, the less he can accomplish.

Every phase of the environment will produce an impression upon the mind; every impression made upon the mind will count. Therefore, in conditioning the mind we must impress upon it everything that we wish to see developed. We need not hesitate in producing too many impressions as long as the mind is interested, for there is no danger of cramming the mind. The mind is highly sensitive to every impression that enters consciousness; therefore, keep out ridicule and discouragement, for what is impressed upon the mind usually continues all through life, unless removed later on by some special method."

The Wizard stepped back from the C.I.M's screen and stood for some minutes, reflecting on the words of Larson. "It's just a shame that he was before his time," he sighed. (The Wizard had learned of the wisdom of Larson by means of a manuscript entitled *The Learning Block* in which another Doctor—a Dean E. Grass—had noted that Larson's theories unfortunately predated many educators' interest in the workings of a child's mind).

Still, there was work to be done and, although time was most certainly on the Wizard's side, he didn't want to waste it. This in mind he set his long shanks in motion, sweeping up the circular stairs in a billow of robes, heading for top landing.

"Elf?"

"Elf!" The wizard stood at the edge of the stairs, looking down as they spiralled back towards mid-landing.

"Coming!" wheezed Elf, one small hand and a green booted foot coming into the wizard's field of vision as his small assistant rounded the last corner. They were approaching the tapered top of the tower, and as the space decreased the magic became ever more powerful. The top floor of the Wizard's abode consisted of a short torchlit corridor, ending in both directions at a stout looking wooden door. The door to their right led off into the Wizard's private apartments, a small and homely suit of rooms where the tower's owner turned in for a good nights rest. To the left, the remaining door separated top-landing from the heart of the tower's magic: the Time Room.

"Are you ready?" The Wizard paused, one hand curled around the doorknob.

"Well . . ." said Elf, looking somewhat sheepish. He had been in—or rather *through*—the time room twice before and while the experience had had hardly been what could be called unpleasant, it was unnerving. All that sliding through time and relative dimensions in space made Elf dizzy.

"Well?" said the Wizard, "Well, if you don't want to come along, I'm sure we can find lots of suitable tasks for you to do around the tower. That is, of course, if you trust me with our bet." The Wizard winked at Elf.

"Erm," Elf's eyes drifted down and to the left as he held an internal dialogue, "I think that I'll come along. It's good to get er, out, I suppose. Not, of course that I think you would cheat in the bet or anything oh great and mighty W . . ."

"Yes. Good, good," the Wizard's hand turned and the door swung open cascading a deep blue light into the corridor. Elf brought his hand up to his eyes, squinting as he shielded them from the bright blue light. The wizard himself seemed to change as Elf looked on. The light alternately making him seem older, then younger, then older again; repeating a cycle of appearance. His robes shimmered, resonating with the newly released blueness, they seemed to merge with the room, making the Wizard fade as he stepped forward into the door frame.

"Let us pay a visit to young Timmy, come; let us fly in the River of Time." Without looking back at his small sidekick, the

Wizard of Was stepped into the Time Room. Elf, now that he was committed, got his little legs moving and followed his boss just as the oak door was beginning to swing shut. It clicked to with a solid clunk, leaving the tower empty. Sending both Wizard and Elf on their journey into the world of young Timmy Watch.

"Ssh!" said the Wizard. They were standing in the back right corner of a school classroom, partially obscured by a large store cupboard but almost comically visible in their outlandish clothes.

"But they can't hear us—or see us for that matter. You know that sir, so what's the point in shushing?" Elf looked up at the Wizard, sure that for once his logic was infallible.

"Yes, Elf. I *do* know that—but we are here to observe and learn. To focus on what is happening around us in this, the seventh year, of Timothy Time's life. We are—or to be more accurate—should be shushing so that we can hear. If you do get the urge to interrupt, try breathing out when you hear them speaking, then you might begin to learn something. There's not any chance that you are trying to put me off winning this bet, is there?" The Wizard raised a suspicious eyebrow at his little helper before turning his attention back to the classroom.

"What? No! I was just saying . . ."

"Ssh!" The Wizard didn't turn his head, so Elf couldn't swear to it, but an ominously serpentine quality had snuck into the shushing and Elf came to the wise decision that now would be a good time to be quiet and pay attention.

The room was average in every way: size, shape, and content were all synonymous with classrooms everywhere and every when. This one only differed in two ways. The heating was up too high creating a somnambulistic miasma of stuffy air, and—even more unusually—the twenty or so students were all paying rapt attention to what was going on. The students sitting at their desks were all looking at one boy who was standing at the front of the class.

"Yet Again, Watch. For the umpteenth time, I'm compelled to single you out as an example for the whole class of what *not* to do in my lessons!" The teacher, Mr Moody, passed a slightly unsteady hand through his thinning, side parted, grey hair. Spots of hectic red had risen in his cheeks and a cold fury emanated from his narrowed ice blue eyes.

Young Timmy Watch, looking every one of his seven years, stared hard at the floor and fought to hold back the tears. He knew that Mr Moody was right. This was indeed the umpteenth time this term that he had been caught daydreaming and at his teacher's words, Timmy's mind became a maelstrom of misdeeds, remembering every single harsh reprimand he had received. No matter how hard he tried to concentrate on Mr Moody's words Timmy couldn't help his attention drifting to the view outside of the classroom window. It wasn't that there was anything particularly fascinating to look at out there. It wasn't one thing at all, it was everything put together than conspired against Timmy's attention span, everything that conspired to turn Mr Moody's stiletto rasp into a nightmare lullaby dragging Timmy's eyelids shut and his attention elsewhere.

"How many times must I tell you? At least have the decency to live up to your name and pay visual attention to me, even if you find my lessons too painfully intellectual to listen to. You're hardly a Rolex are you Watch? I'd like to say Timex but you aren't even that. You, boy, are a faulty knock off, a cheap copy of all the precision and skill that a real quality timepiece exhibits." Timmy risked a quick look up at this infuriated nemesis of his fledgling school career then stared back at a floor blurred by burgeoning tears.

"Well?" Mr Moody looked expectantly at Timmy, causing him to worry that he had again drifted off and missed some all important question.

"I . . ." Timmy began, but the very thought of Mr Moody's cold glare sent icy winds through his mind and he looked again at the floor.

"Why Watch? Why just say 'I . . . um?' what hope do you have in life if you can't even speak boy! I worry about your future I really do. In fact, I suspect that you have so little brain power that if you were twice as clever as you are now, then you'd be a halfwit!" Timmy lost his inner battle and tears tumbled down his hot shame filled cheeks. Mr Moody considered the pathetic child in front of him for a minute, something in his cold eyes softening infinitesimally. "Go back to your seat boy." He said more softly then, softer still, "Go back to sleep too, you're not learning anything here."

"And I thought that you were bad." Muttered Elf, adding a cheeky widening of his eyes in case the Wizard took him too seriously.

"Indeed." Said the Wizard, "Come. We've seen enough here, let us once more take to the River of Time and paddle downstream to a different place. A time a little forward in young Timothy's life."

The Wizard put a guiding hand on Elf's little shoulder and led him to the classroom's stationary cupboard as Mr Moody resumed his tedious lecturing tirade. Partly thanks to the Wizard's wonderful magic, and partly due to the combined effects of the teacher's voice and the room's heating, no one noticed the stationary cupboard door creaking open then shut as the two visitors left the scene.

"Is that the same human?" Elf stared with incredulity at the lanky boy picking his way through the piles of junk covering the wasteland. A gunmetal grey sky squatted overhead heralding the onset of a dark December day.

"Yes, that's a teenage Timmy," the Wizard watched as Tim, head down and shoulders hunched (against either the weather or the world, or maybe both; it was hard to tell) approached the spot where the invisible pair stood.

"Where's he going?" Elf could detect no discernible route in Timmy's wandering. He seemed to be meandering at will through his surroundings.

"Now that is a very good question my little friend. I think that it's time we took Timmy out of the timeline for a while. Got him to walk the purple brick road. Time that we take him to . . ."

"Monster!" Elf suddenly shrieked, interrupting the wizard and running to hide behind his robes.

"Elf! Where? What in the name of all the clocks are you talking about!" The Wizard looked cautiously in the same direction as Elf. Monsters, whilst certainly discussed in the wizarding community, were very rare (and often misunderstood) creatures. The Wizard doubted that he would see any in their current place and dimension.

"There! It's stalking Timmy!" Squeaked Elf, "Look at the size of those teeth!"

Now the Wizard saw just what his miniature sidekick had spotted and a sigh of mixed frustration and exasperation escaped his lips. "*That*, you dolt of an elf, is not a monster. That's a dog"

"A what?" Elf had lowered his voice to a whisper. He knew that humans couldn't hear him, but this monster—this 'dog' thing—not only had the large and threatening teeth of a carnivore but also suspiciously large and floppy ears. Who knew what it could pick up with those.

"For times' sake Elf. You don't have to cower and whisper. It doesn't know we're here, and even if it did, it is a perfectly harmless domesticated creature.

"Even with those teeth?" Elf had stopped whispering but still hid behind his protector's robes.

"Yes. Even with those teeth. Now shut up and concentrate—look Timmy's almost on the purple brick road." Sure enough, as Elf looked, he could make out the spot not far ahead of them where the sparse rubbish strewn grass came to an end and the way to the Wizard's world began.

Timmy didn't notice the difference at first. His eyes were cast downwards, but downwards and to the left as he plodded along deep in his own world of internal dialogue. Slowly, as he refocused on his surroundings, the teenager noticed that something—everything—was different. The ground under his battered trainers had been replaced by what looked like a road of meticulously made and tightly packed purple bricks. The landscape on either side of him had changed too; gone were the piles of discarded household junk, flotsam and jetsam; in their place Timmy saw fields of golden crops waving slightly in a light breeze.

The teenager came to a stop and looked behind him. He could still see the familiar territory of his neighbourhood dumping ground; a grubby stretch of abandoned land where people came to illicitly dump what they no longer needed, a place where no one looked at anyone else. A place where Timmy felt at home. It looked different now, like the everyday world had been coated in bubble wrap, opaque and distorted. The boy took one tentative step back the way he had come, towards the world he knew and then stopped as he heard a bark behind him. "Tock?"

"Woof!" The dog had not turned to follow Timmy, instead trotting further up the strange purple path before stopping and looking expectantly back at his master.

"Tock! Where are you going? C'mon you stupid mutt, lets go back to the waste ground. We dunno what's up that weird path. C'mon." Tock the dog, normally the most faithful of sidekicks (and in Timmy Watch's opinion the only one in his life who always listened to him) took a hesitant step towards Timmy then stopped and, turning again, started to pad slowly up the purple brick road. "Tock!" Timmy repeated, "What's got into you?" The boy shrugged an exasperated huff and followed Tock up the strange coloured road.

"Why is that thing with the teeth coming too?" Elf in his terror at the approaching dog had forgotten one of the Wizard's cardinal rules and not only asked the dreaded 'why' question but also stuck his index finger out in a terribly accusatorial manner.

"Elf!" exclaimed the Wizard.

"What?" said Elf, first warily eying the dog—then going redder than any little green elf had the right to go—after realising what he had said.

"It's bad enough that you've been 'whying' without adding to the insult by pointing *that* at me." The wizard hissed, "You know

30

better than that you really do. I know that forgetting is easy but you are a magical creature after all."

"Ooh!" said Elf, his eyes looking down at his still pointing digit, "How did that happen?" he stared at the finger angrily, as if it had poked out all by itself.

"We'll discuss this later. It's time for Timmy now."

Elf let out a double lungful of air in relief, hoping that the Wizard would have forgotten naughtiness by the time they had dealt with the boy. Then his expression merged back into worried consternation once more as he noticed that the Wizard's wand was in his right hand.

"But I do think that we should take digital temptation out of your way don't you?" With a flick of his wrist the Wizard performed his spell and slid the wand back up his sleeve. For a second Elf wondered what his master had meant by those mysterious words before noticing the strange feeling in his right hand. He looked down in dismay at the funny number of fingers he had left and was about to voice a vociferous protest before he noticed both the Wizard's expression and the proximity of young Timmy watch who was staring at both of them with his mouth hanging open. "You'll get it back later . . . if you ask the right questions." Whispered the Wizard, before turning his attention to Tim.

"Hello Timothy," The Wizard smiled down at the gawking boy. "I am The Wizard of Was, and I'm here to show you how to put right what once went wrong and make what you want to happen."

"You're who and you do what?" Timmy looked down at Elf who was still crouched behind the Wizard's robes, alternating his querulous glance between his finger —missing fist and the alarmingly close teeth of the dog-thing. "And what's that?"

The Wizard looked down at Elf before turning to Timmy and smiling, "Oh don't mind him Timothy. He's my little friend—a bit like your dog really."

"Oh right. Well it looks funny." Timmy Watch stared at Elf, who glowered back sullenly.

"So Timmy, how can I help you?"

"I didn't ask you to. No one can help me anyway." Timmy stared at his scruffy trainers.

"Then can you help yourself?"

"Nope. I'm stupid." Timmy looked around him, trying to recognise a landmark or road, but all he saw were the purple road with its two exotic occupants, Tock (who was eyeing up the guy in the pointy hat's funny bald dog), and the fields of barley drifting off, as if following the course of the road, down a gently undulating hill and towards what looked like a distant river.

"Ah! You think that you are stuck in being stupid. Hmm, I understand."

"I am stupid."

"Yes, I can see what a terrible problem being stupid was for you. Now you are 'stupiding.'"

"Stupiding? I don't see how you can say that, it ain't a word?"

"Ah, it is a word if I say it and you can see it. What does 'stupiding' seem to you Timothy?"

"It makes me think about being stupid instead of feelin stupid." Timmy grudgingly had to admit that he didn't feel quite as stupid as he was once told he was. The four strange companions had been (unbeknownst to all but the Wizard) walking as they talked, heading down the gently slope that wound the purple brick road to the now not so distant river. As Timmy's awareness of how close they were too this strange looking river grew in his head, he realised that he could hear it—not the normal sound of running water but more of a strange hum, a sound of such alien vibrancy that Timmy wasn't sure if he was actually hearing it or not.

"Do you know, Timothy, that it's easy to misunderstand things, to be misled by people who, very often accidentally, tell you something that isn't true. It can make people scared to fulfil their potential, to overcome their problems. We call it F.E.A.R.—False Evidence Appearing Real. Do you know what future you would like Timothy?"

"Maybe." Timmy looked at the Wizard, then back at the strange river ahead of them. It was very close now, close enough for young Master Watch to see the deep silver of its waters, the steady fast flowing stream of its path.

"I see you are looking at the river. The Wizard looked at Timmy and smiled. "That is The River of Time. Fascinating is it not? So . . . there, yet not there."

"And that river is goin to show me how to not be stupid in my future is it?" Timmy asked with a mixture of suspicion and hope in his voice.

"Not the River itself," said the Wizard, stopping by the riverbank and directing Timmy's gaze to the first of a series of five stones that stretched out to the far bank.

Timmy stared at the stones, then at the strange 'water' that flowed around them. His dog too, seemed to share his reticence—Tock had developed a newfound affinity for Elf and the two of them were keeping a healthy distance between themselves and the strange silvery liquid. "I dunno. This river looks risky."

"Time can be tricky, that much is true," said the Wizard in a thoughtful voice. "But in my hands you will be safe on your journey.

"Well," said Timmy, "I do want to see my perfect future."

"You can, the answer lies out their, in time; in your future perfect. Shall we go see?"

"Yeah" muttered Timmy and before he could have second thoughts, the Wizard had snapped his fingers and the two of them disappeared in a puff of purple smoke—much to the consternation of the on looking dog, who barked furiously until he realised that his master and the strange man had reappeared—seemingly unharmed, standing on a stone which looked to be perfectly central in the river.

"We are in your present, Timothy. How do you feel?"

"Funny . . . This whole place is so . . . just not real."

"Yet in a way it is all that *is* real. The past and future Timothy, well they are memories and things yet to be decided, but the present. Well the present is our reality now. Where would you like to be Timothy? What's your future perfect? Would you like to see?"

"Yeah" said Timmy, and with another flash, accompanied by barking from the bank, the Wizard and Timmy reappeared on the farthest away stone from Tock and Elf, the stone closest to the far side. Timmy looked around at the world he suddenly saw with an expression of amazement that soon gave way to a grin of pure pleasure, his face lightening up as it hadn't for years, surprised muscles dragging his lips up into a grin.

"Is that really me?" Timmy turned to the Wizard, indicating to a still young but definitely adult Tim, seen in his future perfect surrounded by a boisterous pack of tail wagging mongrels, trying to wrestle them out of the way long enough to put food in a series of bright steel dishes.

"Yes Timothy, that's you. What do you think?"

"I work in a dog shelter? Kinda cool I guess." Timmy was still smiling but the wizard detected something more, a deeper level of desire in his perfect future.

"Look closer at your future self" Timmy looked at himself again and was just beginning to wonder what the Wizard was hinting that he should look at when he noticed the t-shirt. It had looked very ordinary at first, which is why Timmy hadn't noticed it. A standard faded blue t-shirt with some white letters emblazoned on its back. Timmy leant closer and read 'Watch's Wildlife. Putting pets together with people.'

"I *own* an animal place . . . cool!" Timmy's grin had gotten so wide that the Wizard suspected there was very little need to ask the question but ask it he did anyway, just to be certain:

"Is this where you see the successful you being in your future perfect?"

"Yeah" said Timmy.

"And you look back, back across the River of Time, and to the place where we stood when we met—your then present—the stone in the middle of the River; if we look back from here, the perfect future to the present of now . . . Then can you see Timothy can you see how you got here?"

Timmy's eyes seemed to mist over themselves as he stared back into the River, back to where he was now. "I believed in myself." He whispered. "I believed in myself enough to follow my dream and do what I love. I found out what I needed to do to get where I wanted to be and then I figured out how to get there . . . and it's all because . . . because I now have the confidence that comes from 'knowing where you want to be.'

"From being able to see how the future can lead to the future perfect." Said the Wizard joining in with Timmy's infectious smile.

"Yeah its simple really isn't it!" Timmy was still staring back down the line of time with amazement.

"Inspiringly simple Timothy." Said the Wizard, "I think it's about time that we got you back to your present young Timmy. You've got work to do and, besides, it looks like your dog is getting hungry.

Timmy strained to see Tock standing across the shimmering river on the other bank and indeed, although Timmy couldn't be sure that it wasn't an optical illusion, Tock did seem to be licking his lips. "Yeah, I spose."

The Wizard clicked his fingers one more time and they both disappeared, the Wizard materialising next to Elf on the river bank and Timmy shaking his head in wonderment as he picked his way back through the piles strewn across the wasteland, faithful dog at his side.

"C'mon Tock we've got things to do. We haven't got time to be stupid." A piece of paper dangled from Timmy's left hand, a certificate that was curiously new yet old. It simply read "With Love from the Wizard of Was."

"Borrowed brains have no value."

Yiddish proverb.

"I never came upon any of my discoveries through the process of rational thinking."

Albert Einstein.

"We can easily forgive a child who is afraid of the dark: the real tragedy of life is when men are afraid of the light."

Plato.

Chapter Three

There's a Time for Work

"If you go to work on your goals, your goals will go to work
on you. If you go to work on your plan, your plan will
go to work on you. Whatever good things we build
end up building us."
Jim Rohn.

"I've told you Elf, it's not here!" The Wizard shooed his little helper away from his robes.

"I'm not hiding from *that* one," Elf said, thinking of Timmy's dog Tock. "I was just checking that there weren't more of them."

"Dogs? But we are home Elf, back in the tower, back in the Central Information Room to be precise. Why would there be dogs here?" The Wizard waved an expansive arm and Elf followed its trail, looking up and around. Sure enough, this did appear to be the C.I.R. with its high walls, charts and paraphernalia.

"I didn't realise this is where we were going," Elf looked sheepishly down at his toes for a second, before his attention switched to his now three fingered right hand. "Er," he said, holding the hand up, "any chance of getting my finger back?"

"Yes, yes, of course Elf. I told you; as soon as you ask the right question the finger shall be yours once more."

"What is the right question, then?" asked Elf.

"Then is not the right question." The Wizard walked over to one of the C.I.R's walls and consulted a very large and detailed map.

"Well what is?!" Elf sensed the Wizard's attention refocusing on the C.I.M and was hurriedly trying to get the finger issue resolved whilst he had a chance.

"What indeed." Said the Wizard, his attention still focussed on the chart, "but the question is not what."

"Aaargh! Then what is it if it is not what?" Elf's eyes had almost crossed with the frustration.

"You shall find the answer in time. Right now we have more important things to attend to. So we are agreed that the Time Technique helped young Timmy then?" The Wizard looked questioningly at Elf.

"Well . . . yeah," Elf thought for a minute, "it's amazing how much happier Timmy looked when we left him."

"Yes, it's great is it not?" the Wizard smiled, "just by picturing himself where he wanted to be and bringing that knowledge back to his present means that Timmy now knows what goals to set to reach his future perfect which, incidentally, also freed him from the detrimental block that his memory carried of a bad teacher, allowing him to change this image and its associations of failure from the imperfect to the perfect, putting it to peace in his completed past. Great!"

Elf looked up at the Wizard, "Yup I admit it boss, you got me there. Timmy's certainly better off, but what about the rest of his family? I still say that The Time Technique can't help them all . . ."

"Oh ye of little faith," said the Wizard with a wink, "time will tell."

Elf nodded his agreement and walked over to the Central Information Machine. Its display screen was once again showing the Five Freedoms of Virginia Satir and following the same tactic as he had the last time he'd operated the controls Elf stabbed at buttons until he had randomly selected Tania Watch as his next challenge to the Wizard's technique.

"Ah! Tania!" exclaimed the Wizard, "an interesting choice again Elf." Once again the wizard stepped back to let the C.I.M's information screen change from its list of the Watch family:

> *"Imagine life as a game in which you are juggling five balls in the air. You name them—work, family, health, friends, and spirit—and you're keeping all of these in the air. You will soon understand that work is a rubber ball. If you drop it, it will bounce back. But the other four balls—family, health, friends, and spirit are made of glass. If you*

> *drop one of these, they will be irrevocably scuffed,*
> *marked, nicked, damaged, or even shattered. They*
> *will never be the same. You must understand that*
> *and strive for balance in your life".*
>
> Brian Dyson.
> CEO Coca Cola enterprises.
> 1959-1994.

"These, Elf, are the views of one who knows the world of work well, for he ran a Corporate Giant." The Wizard read the words reflectively, nodding in agreement.

"A Giant!" said Elf, looking fearful, "was it very big?"

"Oh, yes. Big enough to cover the whole Earth. Yet Brian Dyson still recognised the need to keep perspective. Life is a juggling game, Elf. How does one keep all of Mr Dyson's balls in the air without scratching, scuffing or—Wizards' forbid—breaking one of them? That's the puzzle, Elf.

"Are you ready for round two?" asked the Wizard.

"Yes . . . at least I *think* so." Elf crossed his remaining fingers and waited for the magic to begin.

"It's Intercomp on line three. Asking for Tania and chasing up that cash advance for the keystone project?" Sam Scuttle's eyebrows rose as he announced his statement/question to Bernice the receptionist who occupied the opposite desk. Bernice mouthed something back to him and Sam's eyebrows dropped into a furry line of concentration as he strained to make out what she was saying.

"I'll just find out for you Jeff." Sam put the caller on hold and turned his full attention to Bernice. "Huh?"

"Unavailable," said Bernice. "I was saying 'Unavailable,' in that that is what she is." A peel of laughter broke out in the office and Sam and Bernice turned to see a loose group of the office staff standing around the drinks machine and sharing a joke over weak coffee. They were partially obscured by the stacks of boxes that lined the walls and sprung up in irregular columns on any spare floor space some leaking reams of paper that competed for space. Bernice leaned further back in her chair, following the stares of the coffee machine posse.

"Ah," a small scowl of indulgent disapproval crossed her features, "its Dave. He's doin' battle with that printer again." Bernice winced as a cascade of profanity emanating from Dave rolled over the office. The coffee machine posse hooted their sympathy for Dave's dilemma.

"Right." Sam stared down at the slow blinking hold light on the telephone, "that's what I'll tell Intercomp Jeff then, shall I? 'Unavailable'."

"Yeah, I guess," Bernice smiled at Sam before beginning to tap enthusiastically on her keyboard.

"Jeff. Hi, yeah. The thing is, Tania has a very tight schedule for today, so unfortunately she will be unavailable for the rest of the day. Can I take a message? Get her to ring you back?"

Sam nodded at whatever Intercomp Jeff was saying on the other end of the telephone and then said his goodbyes. "She still stressed then?" Sam looked at Bernice who had abandoned her enthusiastic typing in favour of a nail file.

"Yeah! Majorly so." Bernice's eyes swivelled to a glass door that had 'Executive VP Marketing' stencilled onto its frosted upper pane. "She's still in there with *them*."

"Yeah. Senior management from head office. Rather her than me, I'd hate to be scrutinised by *them*. Sam joined Bernice in staring at the frosted glass door, through which he could dimly make out the silhouettes of three seated figures: his boss Tania Watch and her bosses, the mysterious 'senior management from head office.' For a fleeting moment, Sam thought that he could make out two more silhouettes, these ones fainter, more ephemeral, one tall and pointed, the other the size of a small child. Sam stared hard at these new silhouettes but the harder he stared, the more diffuse they became, until eventually they disappeared altogether.

"And I thought that Timmy looked unhappy, but look at *her*!" Elf's curiosity had got the better of him and he had walked up very close to Tania Watch, his nose mere millimetres from the left hand arm rest on her chair. He was staring up at Tania, watching the hectic red of her face, watching the pulse of her carotid artery. Elf turned to look at the Wizard, "I think that this one is ready to blow!"

The Wizard, who had stayed further back to observe the meeting from a more panoramic perspective by the room's window, looked at the two people sat opposite Tania—the gentlemen from head office—to Tania herself and nodded, "She certainly is under an immense amount of stress. Sadly it's an all too common phenomena in the work place, one that has a terribly detrimental effect upon the atmosphere."

"The atmosphere?" asked Elf, now staring at the two men, one fat one thin, sat opposite Tania.

"Yes, it's one of the easiest ways of telling how well a work environment—an office for example—is operating. Work stress has been known to lead to a definite drop in temperature in the office and between colleagues, and pressure and stress are intrinsically linked too."

Both Wizard and elf were now looking over at the three people sat around the office desk. The thinner of the two head office bigwigs was talking to Tania in low solemn tones. "You are still significantly behind the productivity targets that the board stressed were imperative to the turnaround of the company Mrs Watch."

"Yes . . . yes I'm aware of that Mr Stimpson. We are still in the delicate transitional phase of restructuring the corporation. I am confident that we can implement all the discussed alterations to the business plan in time. And please, call me Tania." She gulped.

"Your confidence is all well and good, Mrs Watch." Mr Stimpson's face was solemn; as if the very mention of being on first name terms with this regional office underling represented a professional faux pas. "But I don't think that you understand the seriousness of the situation. We simply cannot afford to overlook the worrying lack of performance that this office has produced since your arrival here as Chief Executive."

Tania watched the austere faces opposite with a mounting sense of dread, her face deepening to an alarming shade of red. Elf's eyes widened with surprise at how stressed she was becoming and he threw a worried glance at the Wizard. The Wizard, though, sent him back a confident wink and returned his gaze to the scene unfolding in front of the two of them.

"I know," said Tania, "that there have been significant problems since I took charge here, but surely you can see that they are rooted in the past management's erroneous decisions and therefore can hardly be blamed on my policies."

"Indeed." Said the other man sat opposite Tania, whose company I.D. named him as 'Gerard Stuckley: Head of Personnel.' "There are, ahem, several specific issues that we must bring to your attention Mz Watch. The most obvious of which is the state of this office itself." He cast a disparaging eye around the cluttered room before continuing, "It is no wonder that you can't achieve your targets given the chaotic surroundings that you and your staff are working in. There seems to be no discernible filing system, rather a random stacking of boxes and . . ."

"The boxes are on our priority 'to do' list Mr Stuckley. I know they look untidy but they are all filed in order and we've had terrible problems trying to get the computer system to work." Interrupted Tania.

"Ah," said the Wizard, "you can tell from both her body language and her words how stressed poor Tania is about all of this, Elf. She is far from sure about how successful she can be. For example, note her use of the word 'trying'—she is trying to get things done, not getting things done." Elf nodded wisely.

"That notwithstanding," Stuckley replied sternly, "so many aspects of good office procedure have yet to be introduced by you. The head office request of personnel reports have not been finished and even the most basic foundations of your job description—such as the implementation of productivity targets, the requested report on our regional corporate rebranding and acknowledgement of team building exercises have yet to be submitted."

Tania looked down at her desk in dismay, "Well, all of those things take time to implement and I've only been here for, what, three months?" she gulped.

"Three . . . months?" Stuckley and Stimpson said the words together, their eyebrows soaring up their foreheads.

"Yes. It's been about that hasn't it? Well, maybe fourteen weeks I suppose. Let me think, it was, er spring when I joined and now its . . . er . . . let me think." Tania trailed off, her voice sinking to the barely audible.

"Tania," for the first time she could hear sympathy in Stuckley's voice. That, and the unexpected use of her first name, made Tania feel more doomed than any of the sombre statements which had preceded them. "Tania, you've been employed by us here for *eight* months." Stuckley did not elucidate—he had no need to. The dawning realisation of the actual length of time which she had been employed for and her suspension of belief made the whole situation feel suddenly surreal. Tania sighed heavily, her lower lip trembling and with mounting dread realised that she was close to tears.

The grey suited figures of Stimpson and Stuckley blurred with her approaching tears and, as Tania tried to blink them away, the whole room swam out of focus, becoming an indecipherable melange of colour and blur. Approaching the point of a stress related breakdown Tania knew she had little to lose in the respect department and allowed herself what she took to be a visible show of weakness, wiping the tears away with a tissue she kept secreted up one arm of her jacket.

The world crept back into focus and, as it did, Tania's jaw dropped. What she now saw was crystal clear, panoramic yet infinitely more surreal than the distorted image of her bosses which until a second ago had filled her blurred field of vision. Gone were the two men in grey. Gone was the cluttered office with its opaque glass backdrop. Gone was the world she knew and in its place stood an alien landscape, one in which a road made entirely of small interlocked purple bricks wound its way through fields of sumptuous golden barley. Gradually, Tania became aware of her surroundings; noticing the gentle breeze that playfully ruffled her hair, the raucous caw of a circling bird and—most intriguingly—the soothing tones of a whispered voice which sounded like it was emanating from the deepest caverns of her being. 'Walk, Tania, Walk. Walk the purple brick road.' It whispered.

Tania blinked and shook her head hard, trying to make the surreal vision she saw fade away yet still it remained and the voice in her head talked on. "Walk, walk, walk the purple brick road." It whispered. Tania stared out across the new vista, looking down the strange coloured road as it twisted between the undulating barley and abandoning rationale she set first one tentative foot, then the other, on the purple brick road.

"Hello Tania." The old man in the funny hat and clothes—surely a Wizard's outfit that he had got from some fancy dress store—was smiling down at her.

"Hello," replied Tania Watch, quite at a loss for anything else to say. She didn't know how long she had been walking down the strange road (*walking* itself did not seem quite the right description to her, it had felt more like *floating*) but the Wizard man was standing at a sharp bend, where the road dipped downhill and disappeared from view. Tania could hear the gurgle of a nearby river in the background. "Where . . . Where is this?"

"This," replied the Wizard, "is 'Was; my country, a place beyond time."

"Why am I here?" Tania felt no fear, indeed she felt the exact opposite; the beginnings of a state of deep calm descend over her, one coupled with a sense of intense curiosity.

"Why, you're here so that we may find out." Said the Wizard.

"Find out? Find out what?"

"You are here, Tania, so that we may find out how I can help you help you."

"I don't think that anyone can help me," Tania looked down despondently and added in a tiny voice "especially not myself."

"Perhaps." said the Wizard, "Yet if myself cannot help you then maybe my elf can show you how to help yourself deal with those problems that you used to have."

"Your . . . elf?" Tania hadn't quite understood what the Wizard man was saying but she had definitely heard mention of an elf and that was blatant nonsense.

"**Elf.**" the Wizard shouted the word so loudly that it made Tania jump. She was just getting over the shock when a rustling in the barley heralded the arrival of a small and extraordinary looking creature. "Ah there you are. Would you be so kind as to lead the way and show dear Tania here to the River of Time?"

Elf looked up at Tania then along the Purple Brick Road. "Aren't you coming too?"

"Certainly." Said the Wizard, "in fact, I shall be there before we have left here." With that, Elf (knowing better than to over question the arcane musings of his boss) headed off around the bend in the road that led to the River of Time with Tania in tow.

"Where are we going?" They were the first words that Tania had spoken since leaving the wizard. She had, up until now, been busy convincing herself that this . . . this *place* and these, these . . . *people* were all part of a dream (or, she secretly dreaded, a psychotic episode brought on by the stress at work) but as she showed no sign of waking up, Tania resigned herself to this new bizarre reality.

"There," said the funny little elf-man. They were just rounding the bend in the strangely coloured brick road and Tania followed the direction of Elf's stare and saw a distinctly odd looking river flowing in front of them. The water was an odd silvery colour, a colour that to Tania looked so subtle it shifted with the current. Deep silver pools of opaquely swirling liquid eddied against fast running streams of moonlit translucence.

"Are we going to cross that river?" She asked dreamily.

"Yes! We are going to travel along The River of Time and see if we can't help you help you sort out that problem which you once had." The Wizard reached out a hand and took hold of Tania's arm, gently leading her down to the edge of the strange river. From here Tania could see five large and perfectly round stones stretching from bank to bank.

"They are the Stepping Stones, Tania," said the Wizard, following the direction of her gaze. "They are very special, because . . . because they exist in all of us and we always start on the middle stone, for that is our *now*."

"But how do we get there without walking over the first two stones?"

"Ah, but we are already there." The Wizard smiled and looking down, Tania saw to her astonishment that she was indeed now standing on one of the flat round stones.

"But how did I get here?"

"You are here, because you have already walked the stones behind you; they are your past. You can step back onto them, to help you understand and resolve those things which already have been, but you will always return to this stone—your present."

Tania looked back over her shoulder at the stepping stones behind her, those of her imperfect and perfect past, and then she again looked down at the stone she was now standing on. "I don't think my problems, at least my work problems, lie in the past though." She spoke in a quiet, pensive voice.

"No Tania," said the Wizard, I believe that you are right. I believe that in order to help you help you in your current professional situation, we must hop not into your past, but your future.

"But that's just it," said Tania, "I don't know how to. I'm under such awful pressure at work that the future is just a nightmare blur. I'm too scared to think of what might happen tomorrow to even begin to think of a long term way through this mess I've somehow ended up in."

"That's because you are looking at things from where we are now, Tania, your present. But you cannot be happy here, or indeed as you say, see any way in which to progress to where you want to be without knowing where that is."

"How do I do that?" Tania wanted so very much to understand what the Wizard was saying, to know how to see her perfect future—her future perfect—and look back from that happy time to her current now; to look back and see what wonderful solutions had provided the past to her perfect future.

"You have to close your eyes and imagine it," said the Wizard. "Imagine yourself on the final stepping stone, moving across the River of Time and near to its far bank. In that future, as you look back and see what it was like to have had that problem, as you think about it now; if you could make this change for yourself so that you could stop having made that change and see yourself now. What do you see?"

"I see myself happily at work with time on my side. I see all of the changes that I know need implementing in the office up and running. I see the staff, challenged and efficient, thriving in the wake of my leadership plans. I see everything that I needed to do and how to get it done." Tania opened her eyes and looked around, first back across the silvery waters of the river at the four stones leading into the past; then hesitantly at the Wizard by her side. "If only I'd looked ahead earlier. If only I could start from the past not the present."

"Yet every now becomes an instant then as soon as it's known." said the Wizard. "Now think back to the meeting you were in in your now. Try in vain to feel the stress that you were under when this used to be a problem. How does that memory of now feel to you now that you know the future is perfect?"

Tania closed her eyes once more in thought. "Now that there is no stress. Now that I can see the future as I want it to be, I know what the right thing to do in that meeting was—to be proactive; to tell the head office bigwigs the truth and . . . and the reason why time is so important to the organisation and running of a successful business.

The Wizard smiled and winked down at Elf, who had been quietly watching Tania's journey through time. "That's right" he said to Tania, "you've got nothing to lose and everything to gain by adopting a realistic approach to what used to be your professional problems. With time on your side, Tania—with a clear and self referential outlook—you can avoid so many of the pitfalls of the job world. Those who cease to see, those who don't learn, often fail to advance their own and their employees or colleagues careers, turning twenty years of experience into nothing more than twenty times one years training, learning nothing new in the other nineteen years. Erroneous bosses often honestly desire beneficial change but—putting up mirrors instead of windows—they look only inwards; reflecting what is being done and turning company views inside instead of looking out at the vast vista of opportunity and advancement which awaits the enlightened."

"I'm ready now," Tania smiled, nodding at the Wizard and his funny little four fingered friend.

"Yes. Yes you are, you have helped you help you and now you see, don't you. That's right." As the Wizard spoke, the scene changed before Tania's eyes and shaking her head as if emerging from the world's strangest internalised pep talk, she refocused on her now and rejoined her discussion with Stuckley and Stimpson. It was only after they had gone (needless to say with Tania's constructive and honest discourse still ringing in their ears) that Tania Watch looked down at her desk, contemplating the last chance she had been given to turn the company around, she noticed a strangely archaic piece of parchment sat amongst the pristine white papers. It simply read "With Love from the Wizard of Was."

Work is for people who have nothing better to do.
Oscar Wilde.

Many managers dread public speaking,
particularly to their peers . . .
Management Today. January 1992.

Perhaps the very best question that you can memorise and
repeat, over and over, is, 'What is the most valuable
use of my time right now?'
Brian Tracy.

Chapter Four

There is Always Time for Other people

All men and women have an equal need for love.
When these needs are not fulfilled it is easy to have our
feelings hurt, for which we blame our partner.

John Gray.

"Well that seemed to work I suppose." Elf turned to the C.I.M's keyboard and then looked up at the Wizard. "Can I have my finger back now? It might help with typing." He gestured hopefully at the keyboard, waggling his remaining fingers over the keys.

"Really Elf, stop being such a wimp—it's not like you're writing a book, all you have to do is prod a key when I tell you to."

"But that's not fair. It was only that stupid dog thing of Timmy's that made me forget and point in the first place." Elf said, aggrieved.

"If I remember rightly ('which of course I do,' thought the Wizard) you ended up being very friendly with the 'dog-thing' as you call it . . ."

"Yeah, but . . ."

"But me no buts, Elf. Actually I was seriously considering returning the said digit before you came out with your 'Well that seemed to work I suppose'. *Seemed?* You *suppose?* Why, by the rights accorded to me in the timeless wizarding charter I really ought to vanish your tongue as well!" The Wizard looked sternly at his little companion who promptly shut his mouth with an audible clack of connecting teeth.

"Good." said the Wizard. "Now if we've settled your little dramas for the minute, and you're quite finished with your negativity and complaining; then perhaps we can get back to work and continue with the curing of the much accosted Watch family." Elf decided that the wisest policy was to keep his tongue safely locked behind his teeth.

"Good!" repeated the Wizard. "So who do we have left? Terry I believe."

Elf nodded and pointed at the C.I.M.'s screen, which was now showing the words of R D Laing:

> I never got what I wanted.
>
> I always got what I did not want.
>
> What I want
>
> > I shall not get.

Therefore, to get it
> I must not want it
since I get only what I don't want.

> > what I want, I can't get
> > what I get, I don't want

> I can't get it
because I want it
> I get it
because I don't want it.

I want what I can't get
because
> what I can't get *is* what I want

I don't want what I can get
because
what I can get *is* what I don't want

I never get what I want
I never want what I get

"Ah yes," the Wizard read the words carefully. "These, my little friend, are the words of the Wizard Laing. They represent very powerful magic indeed—a web of words that can entrap its victims in seemingly inescapable bounds."

"Aren't they dangerous then?" Asked Elf.

"They can be."

"Then why did the Wizard Laing say them?" Elf's little face screwed up with puzzlement.

"To enlighten." Replied the Wizard. "To warn everyone that such knots could prevent the solution of people's problems. We must continue his good work, Elf. We must help cut the bonds of the double bind. We must follow the teachings of our fellow mages and free people to make choices for themselves.

"Language can be very powerful, Elf. It is what we have used in treating the Watch family members, it is what we use to help people help themselves. Look." The Wizard reached into one of his robes prodigious sleeves and produced a rolled up piece of parchment, which he handed to his little helper.

"It won't make my eyes pop out will it?" Elf peered through the rolled up vellum as if it was a Telescope, giving the Wizard a clear view of one paper framed alarmingly green eye.

"No, but I might, if you don't unroll it and read!" said the Wizard. "Honestly, Elf, when are you going to realise that our magic is good and designed to help!"

"Tell that to my finger—where ever it is!" Muttered Elf as he fumbled the parchment open.

On the Nature of Time for Humans.

Time, as it exists to us, is everywhere and always[1]. We think about it every time we are *late*, or *early*, every *time[2]* that we *wonder* what time it is, or *imagine[3]* where we should, or would, be at that time.

Now, reader, time on a watch, in trance, may *pass quickly* to some people and *move slowly[4]* for others. Other people again may *not notice* time at all, or *not care* that it is passing, or be *completely unaware[5]* that it is there at all.

In time, at a time, *one man* could wonder how a *minute* can seem *like[6]* an *hour*, or an *hour* like a *minute[7]*. Naturally, chronological time and in trance time are like *going into another state[8]*, and this might matter, or might not, or it mattering might not matter at all, as all are just temporal experiences.

Taking a long journey, a person crosses time zones, and *no one has to do* anything at all. *No one has to take notice[9]* of anything or pay attention to something, just relaxing and enjoying the

---

[1]   Truism.

[2]   Bind of comparable alternatives.

[3]   Hypnotic Language.

[4]   Apposition of opposites.

[5]   Bind of comparable alternatives.

[6]   Simile.

[7]   Apposition of opposites

[8]   Embedded meaning suggestion.

[9]   Not having to know/do.

travelling. *Thinking of time[10]*, and its zones, the way it changes can be different from experiencing time changing when travelling, when a person just has to *sit back*, and *relax* and not be in or concerned with time at all, like when your *eyelids become heavy and draw down and you sleep, relaxed[11]*, which is not the same as thinking about time and distances and time zones and crossing through and over them when you can be *in two minds at once*. Thinking about time and *just doing nothing and experiencing[12]* it change.

I remember trying[13] and sometimes not even having to try, and knowing almost exactly what time it is without first looking at the time. After concentrating on something else, a person can imagine, and know what time it is if they are in time, and when you are travelling through time you can know what time it will be when you are back, for a moment, in time. Now, I *can't not[14]* know if this is caused by a state of trance, or caused by knowing; imag*in*ing being *in*tuitive and maybe even being *in*spired[15] about time.

Everyone can remember when they were young, or even not that young, yet not old either, the 'patting your head and rubbing

---

[10]   Suggestion.

[11]   Suggestion.

[12]   Dissociation

[13]   Padding.

[14]   Double negative.

[15]   Embedded meaning.

your stomach at the same time' game. Now it always had a long name yet to everyone it was a simple concept—doing two things at the same time which one person will find difficult and another person will have no trouble doing at all. I don't know if this is best achieved by *relaxing completely*, or by *controlling how much you relax*, or *by not relaxing*[16] at all but never all three at the same time, which could be the same as being at the wheel of a ship, very relaxing when steering across a flat lake or very draining when wrestling against rough seas, which could be seen as meaning that being in control can be very relaxing or very stressful. *Psychologists sometimes remark*[17] that a ship is a mind and the body of water it is travelling upon the world. Sometimes the ship is in a serene place, almost drifting, without effort on a beautifully calm sea, sometimes the ship is buffeted, tossed around in a tumultuous environment which it cannot control but must navigate.

When you are flying, and the long flight, or short (but still long enough to be in a different zone of time) flight, is preparing to land, the captain will tell you what time it is in the place where you now are. This can be relaxing as you know the time, or worrying because you now know the time and you are late for something, or both, or neither of these. Many things aren't worth worrying about at all. When you are travelling and forget all the worry, *breathing slowly and relaxing*, or concentrate on what you

---

[16]   Bind of comparable alternatives.

[17]   Padding.

have to do, *breathing at a quicker rate and relaxing[18], you will still feel more relaxed[19]*.

The Nobel Prize winning writer[20] William Faulkner talked a lot about time, and how it could preoccupy people. In "The Sound and the Fury" one character, Quentin Compson describes the power of a pocket watch given by father to son across generations. Quentin notes that his father passed him the watch saying "I give you the mausoleum of all hope and desire; it's rather excruciating-ly apt that you will use it to gain the reducto absurdum of all human experience . . . I give it to you not that you may remember time, but that you might forget it now and then for a moment and not spend all your breath trying to conquer it."

So measuring time can free a man, by placing him in time and also bind a man, by not letting him move through time. Time can be like fire—something that we didn't invent yet something that we can measure. Something that we can partially tame and use to our advantage but also something that, in its wild, visceral state, if not carefully monitored can run rampant, consuming all in its wake. So when a man looks at a watch face, and notices *those hands[21]*, the second hand sweeping around quickly and *lightly*, the

---

[18]   Bind of comparable alternatives.

[19]   Suggestion.

[20]   Padding.

[21]   Dissociation.

hour hand moving slowly, *heavy*[22] with time, it is the concept of time that he remembers not just the hour.

On the news today, a man said that one of the bells in the clock tower in London—not Big Ben itself, but one of the smaller big bells—has been stopped for repairs. Now when you are in London, or even see it on a film, you can hear the distinctive chiming of the bells, *sometimes closer, sometimes farther away*[23], but always distinctive. This sounds will be changed whilst the affected bell is undergoing maintenance and a man interviewed said he would notice the difference in something that had always been the same, so for lots of people the sound of time can be stored *in there*[24] and *like, many other experiences recalled when the time is right*[25]. To the man interviewed, the sound brought back to him memories that had been forgotten, things stored in the *unconscious mind* [26]where we all keep our store of experiences, so many things that make us us, so many things that can *be brought forward to the conscious mind when the time is right*[27] and we need them the most . . .

"My head feels fuzzy," Elf passed the parchment back and shook himself like a wet dog.

---

[22]   Ideosensory feeling.

[23]   Apposition of opposites.

[24]   Suggestion.

[25]   Implication.

[26]   Seeding.

[27]   Implication.

"That, my little friend, is because you have read a treatise on the nature of time, in the language of time. It was passed to me using the knowledge of a group of very powerful fellow wizards . . . although I have added to it somewhat myself." The Wizard said with pride.

"How does the technique work for everyone in relationships? Don't they all need putting through it if it is to become a way of helping them?" Elf looked at the Wizard.

"All those who wish to be helped by the technique could, indeed, do with using the Technique." The Wizard looked down at his little companion smiling, "The question you have asked illuminates one of the strengths of the Time Technique—its universal applicability. It may be that we shall have to help more than just Terry Watch in respect of relationship issues. Let us go and see, Elf, it's time we visited the Watch family home.

"It's not very, well, tall." Elf eyed the suburban three bedroomed semi with suspicion, taking in its oddly shaped square windows and the uniformity of the leafy street it sat upon.

"I know," said the Wizard, "They are strange folk the humans. They don't tend to live in tall towers like ours. But still, we must brave the odd edifice and see what is going on inside—we have a relationship to examine, remember." The two magical beings passed through the unopened front door and into a spacious living room that was unusually decorated, even by human standards. All of the usual furniture items were relegated to secondary positions around the walls and most of the central and wooden floored area had been given over to two enormous artist's easels which stretched up to the ceiling. Terry Watch was bent over the lower half of a canvas on the left hand easel, all his concentration on the brush in his hand as it moved in delicate circles replacing blank canvas with a green grassy hill.

"Is that him?" Elf asked looking interestedly at the man and his art.

"Yes, that's Terry," replied the Wizard.

"I thought we were going to help him help himself with his relationships not drawing." Elf looked around the room, just in case Tania was hiding behind one of the easels or sat on the sofa pushed against the wall but, as far as he could see, apart from Terry and their invisible selves, the room was empty.

"We are. Have patience my little friend." The Wizard stood and continued to watch Terry paint. He noticed how the man was at peace, exhibiting contentment through his body language, loving his work. Apart from the artist, the Watch house seemed empty, a silence permeated the place that was only occasionally interrupted by the delicate sound of brush on canvas.

"He looks happy to me," said Elf. "I know that the technique has helped Timmy and his Mum, but you could see instantly how upset they were. It was obvious that they both needed help and the timeline situations made the reason they needed help pretty obvious too—but this time you've brought us to a point in time where we are looking at someone who is obviously a mature and happy guy. Happy with his work too, by the look of it; and his tower isn't even that small, even if it is short and well . . . sort of square."

Elf had surprised himself by the length of his comments and braced for an onslaught from his boss, but non came. Instead the Wizard looked down at his little helper with a gleam of admiration in his eye. "You see him well, Elf. The wonder of the Time Technique is that it can be employed simply and effectively on all aspects of a person's life. Truly Terry Watch is happy in his work, content in himself and satisfied with his abode yet relationships can be tricky things. They are full of nuance, issues of subjectivity, binds and double binds; for they by their very nature affect not one but two people, and that interplay is dependent on communication even if the two halves form a compatible whole."

"So we will have to take Tania back to the River of Time too?" Elf asked.

"That may be," said the Wizard, "but let us bide our time and watch. It is only when we see them together that we shall know what their problem is."

Just as Elf felt that he could contain his curiosity no more (and was about to risk the Wizard's wrath by asking what no doubt would turn out to be a pointless question), he heard the sound of a key in the lock. The door closed and soon the sound of female footsteps clicked down the hall and into the living room.

"Oooh! Here she comes!" whispered Elf.

"Shush, watch and listen." Admonished the Wizard.

Tania walked in and flung her purse onto the sofa. She stared at the wooden floor, her brow crumpled in a frown of absolute consternation.

"Hi Hun," Terry spoke without looking up from his painting and was greeted with silence. He lowered his brush, half turning from his painting and looked at his wife. "Ah."

"Huh?" Tania came partially out of her reverie. Her mind was still back at the office, things had been going considerably better since her meeting with the head office personnel had surprisingly (to her at least) resulted in a stay of professional execution. She was more than glad that she had a chance to keep her job and now felt very proactive in implementing the changes which she felt were necessary for the resurrection of her company's fortunes; but those changes were still a challenge, and had left her with many a tough decision to ponder.

"Ah." Repeated Terry.

"'Ah' what?" Tania's mind had left the office and was now considering the strange reaction of her husband to her return home.

"I recognise that look." Terry's mind had gone back to a black day in their relationship many years before, when Tania was pregnant with Timmy and furious with Terry for following his (now successful) career path as an artist rather than holding down a more—as she'd seen it at the time—sensible and secure job.

"What look?" Asked Tania, totally unaware of the mental connection that her husband had made between her initial expression and an old buried bone of contention.

"Don't 'What look' me." Replied Terry putting down his paint brush. "That 'You've screwed up and I've got to suffer look' you use when I've not done anything wrong but not done something right that I didn't know I was supposed to do!" All of the old emotions were surfacing from Terry's subconscious and he could feel his old defensiveness growing, and with it his anger and resentment. 'Next it's the martyrdom stuff' he thought, 'the bit where she pretends everything's ok but silently sulks and blames everything that might go wrong but hasn't even been thought of yet on me.' There was no way that Terry was going to stand for this rubbish—not again.

"What *are* you talking about?" Tania was beginning to feel angry herself now. She felt that she had enough on her plate at work, without coming home to a surly husband. 'After all,' she thought, 'I've put up with his artistic angst all of our married life and not gone on about it. He makes me so mad!'

"Oh, forget it!" Terry scowled, flinging his brush to the floor and smearing green on the polished wood.

"And there we have it!" said the Wizard. He had frozen time, as was his power, and the large living room hung in a suspended state, with both Terry and Tania staring and glaring at each other like incredulous ice sculptures.

"Hmmm? What have we got?" said Elf. He was so fascinated by the big people's argument unfolding in front of him that he had wholly forgotten the point of his and his boss's journey.

"The reason that we are here." Said the Wizard, pointing at Terry and Tania with a knowing smile. "Can't you now see the power of relationships? Can't you now see how, although they love each other, they still glare with misunderstanding? What should've been a happy homecoming has instead become a heated argument. They are trapped—bound to the past."

"Yes! I see. I see!" said the elf. "So what do we do? Take them to the River of Time and into their future so that they can see how happy they should be?"

"Well, to the River of Time, yes. That is where they shall go, but I think in this instance we shall demonstrate the alternate use of the Time Technique and send them not forward into their future but backwards into their past."

"The Time Technique works both ways then?" asked Elf.

"Yes, it is very versatile. In my opinion the forward use of the technique is most often the better, as it focuses the mind on what can go right rather than on what has gone wrong. Yet it is good to see it work both ways. Sometimes it is necessary to understand what was in order to change what is and what shall be."

"How does it work backwards then?"

"Let us take Terry and Tania along the purple brick road and we shall see." Said the Wizard as the living room vanished in a swirl of mists.

"Where . . . Where are we?" Terry watch looked over the surreal landscape with an artist's eye, which only served to make everything more confusing. The fields of what he was fairly sure were barley blowing in a gentle breeze on either side of himself and his wife Tania were a normal (if especially vivid) shade of yellow, but the road that they were both standing on was an outlandish shade of deepest purple.

"I think I've been here before." Replied Tania in a quiet little voice.

"Here? Before? When?" Terry looked at his wife with a renewed expression of wonderment.

"I don't think that this place has a 'when' as it were. I think, if I understand it rightly, it just 'is' but if memory serves, we can follow this road to a river that is fluid in time—maybe the river is time. I'm not sure. But it seemed to me when I was last here that this place is all things chronological: what was, what is and what will come to be."

"Is it safe to go to this river?" Terry squinted down the purple brick road, trying to make out the mythical sounding river.

"Is it safe *not* to?" The voice spoke subtly, yet with a curious mix of gravitas and humour. Terry turned around in surprise whilst

Tania followed his glance with a growing feeling of delighted anticipation. Terry's eyes widened as he took in the appearance of the two unlikely looking beings that stood in front of him; the large hat wearing and bearded man was looking down at him with an indulgent expression of concerned humour, whilst his small peculiar sidekick was staring up with apprehensive interest.

Terry thought of all the "reasonable" arguments in the world (or out of it) why it should be unsafe to follow the outlandish bearded individual, his bizarre friend, and his obviously befuddled wife to the location of some mysterious river that would be the cure of all their ills, but for the life of him Terry could think past nothing more than the allure of the fields that surrounded him, the gentle gusts of wind and the sense of all pervading calm that emanated from the newcomer.

"Come with me, it's time to see, yes?" The Wizard walked past the humans and, Elf in tow, started down the purple brick road. After the briefest of hesitations the couple followed; Tania with a look of dreamy expectation and Terry casting an inquisitive, yet more guarded, artist's eye over the spectacularly colourful alien landscape.

"This is like a dream, this *is* a dream." Terry thought the words, yet still seemed to receive "That's all daydreaming—indeed hypnosis—is; a dream of ourselves." He smiled as he walked, thinking this through and how it applied to his current 'now.'

"There." They had just rounded a steep, boomerang shaped, curve in the purple brick road and Tania came to a stop, shielding her eyes with her left hand as if against the glare of a slanting sun, and pointing with her right at the River of Time laid out like a silvery snake winding its way through the gently swishing fields of barley. Terry thought he had never seen something look at once so unnatural and yet so obviously right. The River retained a mirage-like quality even as he and Tania drew near to its glistening banks.

"This is where what was, is, and what could be, flows." The Wizard spoke as the couple reached him at the bank and Terry tore his stare away from the silvery surface with a slight shake of his head.

"Why are we here?" Terry was trying to piece it all together in his head: where he had been before this strange interlude in life.

"Let's see where you were before." The Wizard smiled and extended his hands towards the couple who held out there own and, as contact was made, the three of them began to rise upwards, lifted on unseen currents of air as a feather fanned by wind.

"Do you see those stones?" The Wizard asked. Laid out below the trio, in the midst of the River, were the Stepping stones representing the five points of reference in the timeline. Tania and Terry both nodded, looking down at the stone directly underneath them.

"Underneath you is your present. Where you were and are when you came here." As the Wizard pointed down at it, the middle stone glowed faintly. "Do you remember what it was in your present that used to be a problem to you then and brought you here?"

"I'd just got home from work." Said Tania, remembering. "Yes, I'd just got home from work but my thoughts were still there. I was thinking of ways to resolve the company restructuring issues when Terry got all mad."

"I didn't get 'all mad.' I was happily painting away when you came through the door with a face like thunder and . . ." Terry's voice was starting to rise indignantly.

"Ah!" said the Wizard. "It was Tania's expression, then, that made you feel like she was angry?"

"Well . . . yes." Said Terry, "She always pulls that face when she's worked up and I always . . ."

"You always what?" Tania turned to face her husband, "Yes I had things on my mind when I walked through the door but it wasn't about us. Work's going well for me since my recent and wonderful visit to the world of Was, but I've still got things on my mind from time to time!"

"I know. I know all that—it's just that *look* you got when, when something's wrong. You always got that look, and it always makes me feel the same, ever since . . ." Terry Watch paused as he thought back, back to when he had begun to be so annoyed by 'that look.'

"Yes?" Said the Wizard, "Ever since what Terry? Can you go back to a specific point in time when you and Tania were arguing and remember what it was about Tania's expression that upset you?"

"I . . . I . . . no. Not exactly." Replied Terry. "I can think of times when I was upset with her, and I can see that expression, but I can't think of a specific time."

"Ah, well can you rewind the film of your life to the point where a specific incident occurred? Just rewind the film of your life until you come to that point."

"It's hard to separate them; they are all linked together like knots in a long rope." Terry paused for a minute, his mind following the Wizard's instructions and searching back through his memories for that first time. That first time when Tania's expression had become loaded with such emotion.

"Ah!" said the Wizard, "You have done a very common thing there, Terry. A very common thing indeed for people in 'through time' mode. We often organise memories together in a gestalt—a way of grouping memories that makes the collective memory greater than the sum of its parts."

"There!" Terry remembered. "That's when I first began to dread that look."

"When?" Asked both Tania and the Wizard.

"It was years ago," Terry said, sounding surprised. "It was when you were pregnant with Timmy and . . ."

"Ah, then,"

The Wizard watched as Tania too was taken back along her time line. Back to a time when things had been tough for the young Watch couple. Money had been tight to say the least. Tania was yet to establish herself on her chosen career track and, coming up to the seven month mark in her first pregnancy, she was hardly in a position to launch an immediate and dynamic career progression programme.

Tania had felt that Terry, conversely, was in such a position and Tania felt that he should be doing something a hell of a lot more realistic in respect to the young family's finances than be producing a few paintings that might—or might—not sell. Yet they were a young couple, and Tania could see a bright future for her artist husband—she did not want to be the one who spoiled his dream. So she said nothing, but as the baby's birth loomed closer and the last of the money drained from their bank account that vision of a bright future dimmed in Tania's mind. She still held her tongue but this lack of communication only served to deepen her worries and she resorted to looking at Terry with a mixture of angst and annoyance.

And it was this look that Terry would see every time his young wife walked into the room, every morning when he opened his eyes. The awful thing for Terry was that part of him agreed with Tania, part of him agreed with that accusatory look. For Terry had doubts himself—doubts about being a good father, a good husband. Doubts about whether he would be able to meld his twin dreams of painting and family life. That non verbal 'why?' in Tania's expression had become an anchor so powerful that it triggered a gestalt of memories. The feelings that these produced were so powerful that Terry was unable to free himself from the past and fully take advantage of his great Now and brilliant future.

"So you now know, do you not, that this—this string of memories anchored on a negative event and emotion—is what made you feel the way you did when you saw that look on Tania's face?"

"Yes, I do." Terry nodded at the Wizard, at first hesitantly then with more vigour. "Good. By finding the source of your reaction, and by understanding what those memories mean in the context of your life, you have given yourself the choice of how to react to 'that look'." The Wizard smiled back and turned towards Tania.

"And you, Tania. Do you understand that Terry was reacting to your expression and all the associations that came with it—not to you?"

"Yes." Tania looked across at Terry and smiled.

"Oh!" said Elf, blinking. "We're back here then. When is it?"

"It's the same time as last time of course!" said the Wizard. "Now shush and watch!"

"Hi Hun," Terry spoke without looking up from his painting and was greeted with silence. He lowered his brush, half turning from his painting and looked at his wife. "Ah."

"Huh?" Tania came partially out of her reverie. Her mind was still back at the office, things had been going considerably better since her meeting with the head office personnel had surprisingly (to her at least) resulted in a stay of professional execution. She was more than glad that she had a chance to keep her job and now felt very proactive in implementing the changes which she felt were necessary for the resurrection of her company's fortunes; but those changes were still a challenge, and had left her with many a tough decision to ponder.

"Ah." Repeated Terry.

" 'Ah' what?" Tania's mind had left the office and was now considering the strange reaction of her husband to her return home.

"I recognise that look. Things on your mind?"

"That look?" Asked Tania, "Oh, you know me too well. Just thinking about work stuff. Nothing I can't do."

"I know." Replied Terry, putting down his paint brush and winking at his wife.

"What *are* you talking about?" Tania said, giggling.

"Oh, nothing. I was just thinking how good life is." Terry giggled back and hugged his wife. She felt that she had enough on her plate at work, without coming home to a silly husband. 'After all,' she thought, 'I've put up with his artistic impulses all of our married life and not gone on about it.'

"You make me so mad!" Tania said, laughing and play punching Terry in the chest.

"Ow! Watch it!" Terry laughed as his brush tumbled to the floor, smearing green on the polished wood. As Terry bent down to retrieve the brush he noticed a curious piece of parchment under the easel. It simply read "With Love from the Wizard of Was."

Everyone sees what you appear to be:
few experience what you really are.
Machiavelli.

You can stroke people with words.
F. Scott Fitzgerald.

Assumptions are the termites of relationships.
Henry Winkler.

Chapter Five

It's Time to Start Feeling Better Now

Theoretically, every disease is psychosomatic, since emotional factors influence all body processes through nervous and humoral pathways.

Franz Alexander.

"Well!" said the Wizard, "I do believe that that is that!" The unlikely looking duo were walking down the Watch's driveway towards the main road.

"Why are we leaving the human way? And what what is what?" Elf panted, his little legs struggling to keep pace with the Wizard.

"Hmm?" the Wizard looked down at his assistant. "By 'leaving the Human way,' I presume you mean the path? Simply because I wish to, Elf. After all, our work here is done. *That* is the that that is that. We have helped every member of the Watch family and . . ." The Wizard stopped. He stopped speaking, and he stopped walking, his eyes seemed to glaze over, his thoughts far away.

"What is it?" Elf turned to look up at the Wizard. "What's happening?"

"Ah," said the Wizard, "It's the Central Information Machine. It has just drawn my attention back to the tower. Elf, I feel that there may be one final member of the Watch family left to treat. Come, you shall get your wish after all. Let us travel the Wizard way." With these words the Wizard made a (by now familiar) sweep of his purple sleeved arms which sent the two travellers swirling through time and space back to the tower.

"Yes. It's as I thought." The Wizard was looking at the Central Information Machine's shiny screen.

"It's as you thought?" Elf looked puzzled, "I thought you thought that that was that—that our work with the watches was done?" His little green face crumpled in a look of concentration as he stared at the screen.

"Do you want to be missing a mouth as well as a finger?" The Wizard laughed, "That—as you well know Elf—was then and this is now. Read the screen."

Elf glanced at the readout. "It's just the listing of the Watch family and how we've helped them. Look, there's young Timmy, Tania and Terry and . . ."

"Yes?"

"Oh. There's another one, at the bottom of the list. A Tony Watch."

"Yes. Oh indeed! It looks like our work is not quite completed after all. Back we go I think. Back once more to the Watch household."

"But who is he? And what's wrong with him?" Elf was staring at the name Tony Watch suspiciously, as if it might disappear at any moment.

"Ah, yes Elf. Good points! Let us consult the C.I.M and find out." The Wizard turned towards the machine and with expert strokes of his nimble fingers he accessed the data on the mysterious fifth member of the Watch family.

"Who is he?" Elf asked, standing on his tiptoes and trying to peer over the Wizard's elbow.

"He is Terry's older brother—it seems that . . ."

"What does he want to change about his life? Is he unhappy at work, like Tania, or is he having personal relationship issues, like Terry? I suppose that he is too old to go to school, so that can't be it." Elf paused for breath, determined to puzzle out what could be bothering Tony Watch.

"Indeed, Elf, our second Mr Watch could be having any one of those problems. Something has severely damaged his health."

"What, does he have the 'flu?" Elf laughed, "oh well, much as I hate to admit it your High Wizardness, you win the bet. Terry, Tania and Timmy all used the time technique to help themselves."

"And as much as *I* hate to admit it," laughed the Wizard, "I haven't won quite yet!"

"How not? How can we help Tony? Is it his mind that is sick?" Elf looked cagily at the Wizard, suspecting that he had lost the bet and that his boss was just mocking him.

"The body cannot live without the mind, Elf. When the body is sick then the mind is aware; is it so hard to believe that when the mind is sick that the body is aware?"

"Er, I suppose not," said Elf "So what are you going to try and cure him of?"

"Really Elf! You know better than that." Said the Wizard "I'm not going to try and cure Tony Watch of anything. We shall merely show him how to let his mind help his body."

"Minds can do that?" Elf was frequently suspicious when it came to the power of minds—especially his own.

"Yes," said the Wizard, "All of our minds—both consciously and subconsciously—influence our bodies on a continuous basis. Think, Elf, and your body will react. Think of your favourite food; imagine the look of it, the smell, the taste. Are you salivating?"

"Um, yes," Elf (who had been imagining chocolate pudding) gulped.

"Well there you go Elf. You turned a thought in your mind into a physical reaction, salivating. Breathing!"

"Um yes, I suppose I did . . . breathing?" asked Elf.

"Yes, same theory. If you think 'breathe quickly' your physical rate of respiration will change accordingly. A process of thought to bodily reaction. Or, to put it the other way around; fear can be aroused by the memory of pain. Something physical that happened to the body becomes a memory and that memory can translate into emotion. In fact, let us consult the C.I.M on the subject." The Wizard turned back to the machine and a new text glowed on its screen:

The territory of mind-body medicine has no givens and no inflexible rules, which is all to the good. For decades, medicine has known that much disease has a psychosomatic component, yet dealing with that component has been like trying to harness the wind. Inside us there must be a 'thinking body' that responds to the mind's commands . . .

Deepak Chopra. Quantum Healing

"Ah yes, Chopra. He could well be a valuable resource to us, Elf, when we come to help Tony's mind help his body to feel better. He has devoted much time to studying the link between the mind and the body, that conduit which allows a thought to produce a physical response.

"Shouldn't we see what is wrong with Tony then? See who's won this bet?" asked Elf.

"Yes, I think that that we shall do more than that, Elf, I think that we shall show him a way of putting it right. With a wave of his arm the Wizard moved the two magical travellers through time once more, once more back into the Watch family home.

When he lowered the purple arm of his cloak, Elf found himself blinking out into the antiseptic, chalky air of the watch family's spare bedroom (or, more accurately what used to be the spare bedroom until seven weeks ago when Terry's unwell brother Tony had come to stay).

"Is that him?" Elf was craning his neck, peering forward into the gloomy room and squinting at the dim outline of a figure lying on their back in bed.

"Yes, let's go meet him." The Wizard strolled into the room and towards the bed, dragging Elf along in his wake.

"Hello?" Tony Watch moved his head slightly, trying to get a better look at the tall figure walking in through his bedroom door. The normally subdued electric light falling into his room from the landing shone brightly, placing the tall figure into a feature-obscuring silhouette.

"Hello!" said the Wizard approaching the bed with a big smile on his face.

"Er . . . What can I do for you?" Tony was reasonably convinced that he was dreaming. The tall figure had moved forward enough now for Tony to realise not only that the newcomer was a stranger (alarming enough in your bedroom!) but a stranger who was wearing a billowing purple robe. Any remaining thoughts about still being awake left Tony's mind as soon as he spotted Elf trotting along beside the Wizard. He felt curiously calm (a very unusual emotion for Tony under any circumstances) as the Wizard's approach.

"You can let me show you how to help yourself." Said the Wizard.

"How?"

"Close your eyes and I'll show you." As Tony lay back and closed his eyes, his dream changed. The stuffy, medicinally tainted air of the bedroom was replaced by a gentle breeze; the room's walls gave way to fields of golden crops; the ceiling dissolved into the inky velvet of a summer evening sky.

"Where are we?" Tony sat up on the edge of his bed.

"This isn't 'where' Tony—it's 'when'." The Wizard looked Tony in the eye. "There is a place, very near here. A river, *the* river I suppose—The River of Time. If you know how, you can travel across it, and it will take you back to what was or forward to what could be. Would you like to go there with me?"

"I suppose so," Tony was looking less calm, a strained expression draining the colour from his face. "Although, to be honest, I could do with more peaceful dreams than these. I'm not a well man you know."

"I know," said the Wizard, taking Tony gently by the arm, helping him on his first few steps as they began to walk together down the purple brick road.

"What's wrong with him then?" Elf asked the Wizard. Tony was standing a few feet in front of them staring into the fast flowing river so Elf whispered his question, although he needn't have bothered as Tony was steadfastly refusing to acknowledge his existence having decided that this dream was strange enough without Elf.

"Ah, Deepak Chopra writes of this. Tony has become so mentally agitated—so stressed—that it is having a number of adverse affects on his health. In moments of stress and danger, the body halts the digestive system to divert blood to more important functions. In the complex world of human existence, however, stress can be a constant factor and overtime the digestive system can become pulled like a tug-of-war rope between contrary commands to: relax and eat; stay sharp and stressed. Many Stressed people end up with stomach ulcers and chronic irritated colon problems. There's a reason why people talk about being 'sick with worry.'"

"That sounds horrid!" said Elf fearfully

"Every illness is horrible in its own way, yes Elf." The Wizard looked at Tony, who saw still staring into the River. "And the effects of stress, for example, are many. On a purely physiological level, stress releases harmful hormones such as cortisol into the system that, over time suppress the immune system. No wonder Tony is so unwell. Come Elf, let's talk to him."

"Do you feel what the river is?" The Wizard asked.

"Yes." Tony said dreamily, still staring at its waters.

"Do you see where we are now, along the course of the river?"

"Yes I see where we are." Tony's gaze focussed on the central stepping stone in the river.

"Good," replied the Wizard. "Then let us stand on that stone."

"Now as we stand here in your present. Can you look back along the flow of the river to your past?

"Yes," said Tony, looking back along the river.

"Can you remember a time in your past? Tony, can you remember a time, say when you were two years old and no illness had ever afflicted you? Yes? Back then you didn't feel ill, no? A time before you felt so stressed?"

"Yes," Tony's face relaxed, the tension beginning to leave his body.

"Now can you look forward, Tony? Forward into a future where you are free of the health problems that were so terrible when you had them?"

Tony paused, thinking for a minute, thinking of a mystical time in the future when his gut wasn't tied up in knots and his life in danger of falling down around his ears. "Yes . . . Yes I can imagine that." He said, smiling.

"Can you see what was different in your past, and will be different in the future, that stops you suffering as you were in your 'now'?" The Wizard asked.

"Yeah," laughed Tony. "My world wasn't collapsing back then and I didn't want it to still be when I thought of the future."

"That makes sense," the Wizard of Was nodded, chuckling. "What was different about your past and future, which meant that you weren't ill?"

"Well, I wasn't this stressed!" Tony spat the words out.

"Can you see a point in the future when the problems that you had before are solved and you feel less stressed?" the Wizard asked.

"Yes." Tony, with the Wizard, stepped to his future perfect.

"Then that is very good Tony. You have the capability to see a way through your problems then, that is a talent!" the Wizard smiled, "And do you see that the stresses of your life are affecting your health, which is making your life more stressful?"

"Yes. I can see that." Said Tony, "It's not that I want to be stressed, it's just that life's so . . . so . . . so . . . stressful!"

"Yes, I know." answered the Wizard, "It has been said—and rightly—that 'the medical model itself is a set of stressful beliefs. It implies that when you are ill, your body is out of your control and you need to go to experts to be cured. On the other hand, a belief that you are totally responsible for healing yourself and no one can or will help you is also stressful.'[28]

I know that it will take time for things to improve so you must help yourself by relaxing when you can. You believe that

---

[28]   NLP and Health. Ian McDermott and Joseph O'Connor. P132

you can get better. This is a vital belief in recovery. By not being stressed all of the time you will give your body the chance to recover from the troubles of the mind. Can you sometimes put yourself in that future place where you are healthy and the stress has gone?"

"Yes," said Tony, looking brighter once more, "Yes. I do see how I can be less stressed."

"That's Brilliant!" replied the Wizard. "You have done so much to help yourself recover. By recognising that you were stressed and that this was making you ill, you acknowledged that the stress needed dealing with. You have focussed on the stress in your 'now' and developed strategies to diffuse the stress by controlling what you can and letting go of what you can't control."

"Yes, I see now that there is hope in the future." Tony turned from his future, preparing to step back across the stepping stones of time to his present but to his surprise he saw that they were already standing back on the river bank.

"I'll wake up feeling better now." Tony yawned. The three travellers had walked back up the purple brick road and Tony had not been in the least surprised to find his bed just where they'd left it.

"Sleep well, now." Said the Wizard of Was.

Tony Watch woke up from his nap feeling more rested than he had for longer than he cared to remember. Strange images from the dream he'd just been having still hung behind his eyes. Tony stretched and breathed deeply, 'Tonight is not a night for feeling stressed,' he thought, turning onto his side. The bedside table sat, as it had since Tony's arrival, covered with pill bottles and bottles of brightly coloured medicines. On top of the usual paraphernalia rested a curious looking piece of parchment. Tony leant over and picked it up. It simply read "With Love from the Wizard of Was."

"Well?" The Wizard of Was was positively grinning down at Elf.

"Hmm," said Elf. The two of them had left the Watch household as quietly as they had entered it, taking the magically direct route of teleporting back to the Wizard's tower. They were now standing in the Cavernous C.I.R and the elf was once more squinting at the text on the machine's monitor.

"'Hmm', Elf? 'Hmm'? That's all you've got to say? What does the writing on the Central Information Machine tell us?" The Wizard nodded towards the C.I.M.

"I don't know," said Elf looking distinctly uncomfortable. "The letters look funny to me. Maybe it's broken. How would I know? I'm just an Elf . . . and the screen is too high anyway—it's too big. This whole room, in fact, is too big." Elf stared up at the Central Information Room's lofty ceilings.

"Quiet! You are rambling, Elf," the Wizard said, not unkindly. "As you seem incapable at the moment, I shall read the words on the screen."

"No. Really!" Elf started edging towards the rooms large double doors. "It's ok oh mighty mage! It's been fun, it really has, but I've got things to do down in the kitchens."

"Elf! You wouldn't be trying to get out of our bet would you? Not when you were so confident that the Time Technique couldn't help all of the members of one family!" the Wizard waved a hand at his small companion and he reluctantly walked back over to the machine.

"Oh, go on then, what's it say?" Elf suspected that he wasn't going to enjoy losing this bet.

"Your enthusiasm is overwhelming, my little friend," laughed the Wizard, "It is, I am pleased to say, a list of the now familiar Watch family. A random family selected by . . . why, by *you* if I remember rightly!"

"Yes! Yes ok!" squealed Elf, "I admit it! You were right! You win. The Time Technique did help them all. It's wonderful! Everyone should do it! Now, if you don't mind boss, I'll er be going now. I've got things to do—important elf things—and it's not like I'm even missing that finger any more so I'll just get out of your way." Elf was practically hopping backwards towards the door.

"Ah! Yet there is *one* more thing—our bet, Elf. It's time for you to pay your forfeit." The Wizard drew back the sleeves of his robe and began to cast a spell at Elf.

"Nooooooo!" Elf squealed, holding his hands out in front of him, the gap where the missing finger once was did nothing to obscure his view of the chanting Wizard. There was a blinding flash of light and Elf shut his eyes and screamed, almost drowning out the two loud popping sounds that followed.

"Will you be *quiet* and get on with paying your debt to the bet!" The Wizard shouted. He feared that Elf's screeching might just be able to break glass.

Elf shut his mouth with an audible clash of teeth and warily opened an eye. He stared at the hand still raised out in front of him. "My finger! It's back!"

"Well, you'll need it, won't you. To . . ."

"What's with this cloth?" Elf, now with both eyes open, had discovered that his other hand held a large white cloth.

"As I was saying," said the Wizard, "you will need all your fingers to do all the extra work."

"Work?" Elf eyed the cloth with renewed suspicion, his joy at getting his finger back temporarily forgotten.

"Why yes! The terms of the bet. You haven't forgotten have you?" The Wizard grinned at his little helper.

"I'm beginning to guess" Elf said sarcastically.

"Yep. You get to clean the tower for the next hundred years. Again."

"Yeah—again," Elf grumbled, thinking of all the pots that needed cleaning downstairs in the kitchens. "I must stop gambling, and I'm sure he rigged that somehow anyway . . ."

The Wizard of Was smiled as the sound of his little friend's muttering receded down the tower corridor. He turned back to the Central Information Machine and began pushing buttons.

"Right—next!" said the Wizard . . .

"This is to certify that the age old Time Technique is indeed versatile and has helped each and every member of the Watch family with a whole range of problems and issues."

With Love to the Wizard of Was

*Health is the state about which medicine
has nothing to say.*
W.H. Auden.

*Physicians pour drugs of which they know little,
to cure diseases of which they know less,
into humans of which they know nothing.*
Voltaire.

*To enjoy good health, to bring true happiness to one's
family, to bring peace to all, one must first discipline and
control one's own mind. If a man can control his mind he
can find the way to Enlightenment, and all wisdom
and virtue will naturally come to him.*
Hindu Prince Gautama Siddharta,
(The founder of Buddhism, 563-483 B.C.)

> *"Truth is incontrovertible; malice may attack it and ignorance may deride it; but, in the end; there it is."*
> Winston Churchill

A Brief History of the Time Line

Do you have time to read the introductions to books? Do you have time to read this book—even if its aim is to help you to use time to your advantage? Time, you see, is a funny thing. If you wait for it to pass, it seems to slow down almost to a stop. If you try and hold on to it, it slips through your fingers like water or fine sand. Time is something that we cannot escape. We can't see it, yet it has a profound affect on every aspect of our existence. Time and its rhythms run through our bodies with the beat of our hearts, they surround us in the tides, days, and seasons of our lives. Even the Universe itself had a beginning, now long past; has a present; and will ultimately end in the far distant future.

So how do we deal with this tricky concept? The concise version of the Oxford English Dictionary primarily defines 'time' as "The indefinite continued progress of existence, events, etc., in past, present, and future regarded as a whole." This definition aptly elucidates the amorphous nature of time. In total, the concise OED devotes over a thousand words to its definition of 'time'. Compare this to another element of existence that we measure, say gravity, which is succinctly defined in seventy words or, to pick a more mystical example, say God, and the dictionary summates its definition in three hundred words. How do we—as a species—measure something so 'indefinite' as time?

The answer is that we quantify it. Recent medical research conducted on a National Academy of Sciences study at Washington University, and made possible by the introduction of MRI scanning technology, shows that specific areas of the brain are active when thinking about upcoming events. These findings correlate with existing evidence of damage reported in areas of the brain of patients who have lost the ability to think ahead. During the MRI scan, volunteers were asked to 'remember a past birthday" and then to "imagine a future one." When imagining the future, the scan showed increased electrical activity in the left lateral premotor cortex, the left precuneus and the right posterior cerebellum.

Researchers wrote: *"Perhaps one of the most adaptive capacities of the human mind is the ability to fashion behaviour in anticipation of future consequences.*

"Much of our everyday thought depends on our ability to see ourselves partaking in future events."

These recent scientific findings substantiate the beliefs of this book, that the monitoring and manipulation of time are not only fundamental but also comprehensible. In short, we are hard wired to understand time and it's advantageous to understand the programming that goes with that hardware.

The human brain has, from sundials to the atomic clock, a long history of producing ever more portable and accurate means of measuring the passing of time. But how do we see time? What system do we use if we want to see the past, the present and the future all lain out? We use the Timeline.

What is the Timeline? Well, it's exactly as it sounds: time lain out in a line. Academically this provides a standardised methodology for study across many disciplines. Geologists, historians, sociologists, physicists and teachers (to name but a few) demonstrate the passage of time, from what happened in the past, what's happening now, and what is likely to/could happen in the future by means of a simple graph.

```
┌─────────────────────────────────────────┐
│                                          │
│                                          │
│  ─────────────────────────────────       │
│      ┌──────────────┐                    │
│      │ Timeline     │                    │
│      │ x axis       │                    │
│      │              │                    │
│      └──────────────┘                    │
│                                          │
└─────────────────────────────────────────┘
```

Events—for example the life of the Universe—are laid out along the independent value horizontal (x) axis. Uniformly, the left side of the line represents the past (in the Universe example this would start with the Big Bang). The very start of the Universe is now a completed occurrence far in the past. Then further along the timeline, yet still far in the past, would be: the birth of the Sun five billion years ago; the emergence of the earliest forms of life nearly four billion years ago; mammals evolving two billion years ago, and the extinction of the dinosaurs sixty five million years ago.

The arrival of Homo sapiens six hundred thousand years ago—and everything from then up until now—would take up the rest of the timeline to the central point. This central point, exactly in the middle of the timeline, is the present. Events as they are unfolding precisely now. Right of this central 'now' point on the timeline lies the future. Now, by its very definition, we don't know what is going to happen in the future. But by hypothesising—by using our knowledge of the past and our intellect in the present—we can deduce likely events and the time frame of those events.

In the Universe example, the near future—which in the life of the Universe will last for One Hundred Trillion years—encompasses the stelliferous era (the state of the Universe as it is now, with most of the energy being produced by stars). After this, and further to the right of the Universe's timeline, we find the Degenerate era—extending to Ten Trillion Trillion

Trillion years after the Big Bang (and in which the Universe's mass will be contained in collapsed stars). Further still to the right, we find the Black Hole era—Ten Thousand Trillion Trillion Trillion Trillion Trillion Trillion Trillion Trillion years after the Big Bang—in which only the black holes will remain. On the ultimate right of the timeline, we see the Dark Era. After ten to the power of one hundred years of existence, the Universe will have dissipated and only the residual after affects of what once was will still remain.

Hopefully, this example demonstrates the power of the Timeline as a tool. The very Universe itself can be represented, made clearer, if it is visualised in terms of the past, present, and future. It follows then, does it not, that if we, as individuals, think about our own lives in terms of our personal Timelines, then we will gain clarity and control over our pasts, our present and our futures? We do this automatically, if not always consciously. The existence of our internal timeline is reflected in our language. "I remember back when . . ." is a common saying. Have you ever heard anyone say "I remember forward to when I was a small child."? We "look back" on the past; we "look forward" to the future. Even in the world of fiction, it takes the introduction of time travel to alter this rule. (The *Back to the Future* films spring to mind).

So our futures lie ahead of us, and our pasts behind. We record time in this way, and more than that, we calibrate our recording system[29]. Things which have happened recently (or will happen soon) are in the near past (or future). Events which occurred many years ago are described as having happened in the distant past (or as one famous movie put it "A Long time ago in a galaxy far, far away."); again this same use of distance applies equally to the future. Our brains quantify time in terms of distance, with the more recent an event being, the 'closer' it is to us, the more distant event the further away it is.

We can by now begin to understand the process of measuring time both on a societal and individual level, and how useful that process can be for sorting out the maelstrom of events and ideas that constitute our comprehension of existence. This understanding is amongst the fundamental interests of NLP (Neuro Linguistic Programming)—an interest in *process*. Many areas of conventional wisdom, from religion to psychology, place an imperative on forgiveness and the resolution of past problems before you can truly move on to a successful future. NLP endorses this, but where it differs from these other disciplines is in its primary interest in *how* we can achieve these goals.

In terms of the oft mentioned 'nature/nurture' debate—whether we are who we are, do what we do, because

---

[29] Individual Timelines are stored in a wide variety of ways, as will be discussed later in our 'In Time/ Through time section).

of genetic programming or learned behaviour—NLP recognizes that we are all evolved members of the same species, but the most influential factor is our 'nurture,' our learned behaviour, our programming. It is this process that NLP maintains can be actively changed to our considerable benefit. It is the aim of this book to show you how to instigate those changes.

This book builds on an extensive canon of work dealing with the human mind and time. Aristotle noted that "Western minds represent time as a straight line upon which we stand with our gaze directed forward; before us we have the future and behind us the past. On this line we can unequivocally define all tenses by means of points. The present is the point on which we are standing, the future is found on some point in front of us, and in between lies the exact future; behind us lies the perfect . . ."[30] and his musings proved to be both foundation and catalyst to the discipline of psychology.

The late Nineteenth and Twentieth Centuries saw a renaissance of this Aristotelian philosophy. William James, writing in *Principles of Psychology* (1890), stated that in order for the mind to function, the 'constitution of consciousness' consisting of 'a string of bead-like sensations' have to be connected. This idea of interconnected memory grew in strength in the early Twentieth Century with the rise of Gestalt[31] psychology. Academics such as

---

[30]   *Hebrew*, p 124.

[31]   The OED defines 'Gestalt' as being 'an organised whole that is perceived as being more than the sum of its parts'.

Kurt Goldstein realised that the applications of Gestalt psychology could be used in a practical sense to address the problems of time management and personality. Goldstein's ex assistant, Fritz Perl, further developed this approach, splitting from the gestalt psychologists and instead advocating Gestalt Therapy.

The schism that developed between Gestalt psychologists and Gestalt therapists set a pattern which has continued to the present day. In the same way as gestalt psychologists mistrusted the 'hands on' approach of gestalt therapists (despite their mutual academic background) many members of the contemporary academic establishment view NLP as the suspiciously illegitimate progeny of psychology. This split with many elements of traditional academia has not, however, prevented first Gestalt Therapy (Fritz Perl, his associate Jim Simkin and others had considerable success in their field) and now NLP from bringing the fruits of psychological academia to the general public.

In the early days of pre NLP development the foremost hypnotherapist of his time, Milton Erickson (1901-1980) did much to combine the then unconventional and practical. Erickson proved, and developed techniques, demonstrating that hypnosis could fast track therapy by providing a direct communicative route to a patient's subconscious thereby putting people at their ease and enabling them to help themselves by accurately and instantaneously accessing the root cause of their problems. This linked in well with the 'connected memories' theory of gestalt therapy and formed the foundations of the quick and process driven therapy that was to evolve into NLP.

Erickson had a great influence on his academic colleagues and protégés. Indeed he is often quoted by the founding fathers of NLP—Richard Bandler and John Grinder—as being of seminal importance. They realised that the main power held by NLP was its ability to combine hypnotherapy and psychotherapy. In effect this combination allows NLP practitioners to help clients address issues quickly and effectively on both a conscious and a subconscious level.

The prevalence of time related therapy—the study and manipulation of the mechanisms by which we calibrate and interpret time—has gone from strength to strength in the NLP canon. *The Wizard of Was* continues this line and builds upon the firm foundations of Time line Therapy™—a technique developed by Tad James, Ph.D who continues to make breakthroughs in the field (and who, along with: Wyatt Woodsmall, Ph.D; **Bobby G. Bodenhamer, D.Min; and L. Michael Hall, Ph.D, have published widely in the area of time related therapy). Indeed, more and more people are becoming aware of** a technique that enables all of us to access our own internal timelines and use them to our advantage in any area of life.

As well as discussing and referencing this technique as it is used by NLP practitioners, *The Wizard of Was* both suggests new angles on the use of NLP therapy and time; and demonstrates how the technique works in a variety of situations by following the fortunes of the fictional Watch family as they are introduced to their inner timelines by the mystical Wizard himself. So if you have the time, if you want to see the time technique in fictional action, then follow the Wizard of Was on his adventures, and find out a whole lot about NLP along the way. If however, you don't like stories, or you'd like to spend the precious commodity that is time in a different way—but you still want to learn how to turn time to your advantage—then the technique is laid out after this introduction, and also summated before and after each of the story's main chapters.

Time line Therapy.
What it is and how to use it:

So 'How do we see time?' Well, linguistically speaking, if ever there was a case of the clue being in the question then this is it! 'Seeing' time is far easier to do than using our other senses. We do not, after all, 'hear' time, nor do we 'smell', 'taste' or 'touch' it. When ordering our memories and dreaming of the future, we use pictures—images, and often, moving images. NLP refers to this as the use of a visual submodality, most people know 'submodalities' better as 'senses.'

A vast amount of information is stored in our memories of what was and desires for what will be. The visual system is the best way for the brain to catalogue this information as a lot more data is stored this way than by our other senses. As the old saying goes, 'A picture is worth a thousand words.'

You can try this for yourself. Think of something that you have done on a repeated basis in the past—for example drinking a glass of water. Do you remember drinking a glass of water five years ago? Can you remember drinking a glass of water two years ago? Recently? Can you imagine yourself drinking a glass of water in the near future? And in a few years time?

It is very hard to recall an exact memory of doing something mundane or imagine doing it in the future. You most probably got a quite general mental image of yourself performing the act in each instance. The nature of those images is very individual, and includes any number of combinations of the submodalities identified by NLP. Do the images appear in black and white or colour? Are they still or moving? Panoramic or framed as if on a screen? How bright are the images—do they get dimmer or brighter the more distant a memory you recall? Are they sharp or fuzzy? Do you see the memory through your own eyes or are you watching yourself in it? Where in your field of vision do the images appear?

It is these variations that the brain uses to separate memories by age. Of course many of these submodalities are limited in themselves, whilst we may store our images of the past and future framed or unframed, in colour or in black and white, the nature of storing time requires a subtle gradient of differentiation. (NLP categorises this as the use of the more variable analogue submodality rather than the 'on or off' digital ones.) The human brain uses location and distance as its method of separating past, present and future. This importance of the location of memories, and the way that the mind does this unconsciously in order to better access memories sequentially, provides us with the structure of a time line.

The way in which our minds arrange this 'line' is individual and there is no perfect way to do it. There are, naturally, reactions to our actions of storing time the way we do. If, for example, you store your past in front of you, it will be hard to see beyond it—hard to move forward and get see the future you want. Conversely, if you store your future behind you, how will you go forward in life? What if you change the way you store time so that your past lies behind you, clear and recollective? And the future you want for yourself, what if you place that ahead of you, big and bright?

In Time and Through Time:

NLP and Time Line Therapy™ teach that people operate in two different time modes— 'In time' and 'Through time'.[32] Briefly put, being 'In Time' is living in the moment, focussing on the

---

[32]   The concepts of 'In Time' and 'Through Time' are posited by Tad James and Wyatt Woodsmall in their book *Time Line Therapy and the Basis of Personality*.

now, whilst 'Through Time' takes into consideration the future. Time Line Therapy™ suggests a split between Anglo-European Time and Arabic time, essentially arguing that elements of the post Industrial Revolution world adopted the 'through time' mechanism as a means of keeping to work schedules and the chronological demands of the industrialised world. Whilst it is true that the benefits of adopting a 'Through time' approach were fundamental to the technological development of man, it is arguable that our ability to plan ahead is a natural function of survival.

Both human and animal brains have demonstrated the ability to move between 'in time' and 'through time' modes when the situation dictates. A squirrel is planning ahead (through time) when it buries its winter store of nuts, but if it couldn't also make decisions in its present (In time), it would be unable to evade danger. If we are capable of swapping between planning ahead and living in the moment then we reap the rewards of both systems. We get the 'In time' benefits of concentrating on the 'now,' enjoying the moment more fully and worrying less about what might go wrong. If we move into 'Through time' we gain the advantages of planning, punctuality, ambition and foresight.

Characteristics of In/Through Time Behaviour:

Through Time	In Time
Difficulty wasting time as it has a high value.	Perceiver
Love of organisation, calendars, diaries . . .	Ability to put the past in the past—not preoccupied with what has been.
Goal Orientated.	Association with past memories, more visceral grasp of future goals. When in 'In time' mode, we have a more powerful but less objective perspective.
Punctual, Astute, judgemental.	In the 'now'—heightened enjoyment.
Prepared—plan ahead	versatile—adjust to changing circumstances.

Finding your Time line:

So how do you go about finding your Time line? Well, our unconscious mind knows where we keep our pasts, presents and futures, so if we consciously follow the processes of memory recall and future planning then we can find out where they lie.

Try recalling an event from a year ago. Which direction does the image of the event come from? It can be inside or outside of your head. It can be up/down/left or right. Take this book and point it in the direction of that image.

Now imagine something that will most likely happen in a year's time. Pay attention to where this image comes from. Again, it can be inside or outside of your head. It can be up/down/left or right. Take this book and point it in the direction of that image.

Usually the two images—the one from the present and the one from the past—appear in different, often opposite, directions (occasionally they come from the same direction but at different distances).

Close your eyes and picture your present. Is it inside or outside your head?

With any luck you have just said something along the lines of "Oh, yeah!" and now know where your Time line lies. If not, then don't worry, the above technique works for many people, but not all. To firm up your vision of your Time line, or to help discover it if you haven't already (and if you haven't, remember it doesn't matter, your Time line will appear to you when you are ready to see it) try recalling a series of happy events over past years, then imagine happy future events as you cross the river of time. The events should appear along your time line, yes?

If you still can't see your Time line then lets pretend that that you know that you *do* know it deep down. Ask your unconscious mind to take control of your finger. Your unconscious mind knows which finger of which hand to point in the direction for your past. Congratulate your unconscious mind when it points in the direction of the past. Now ask your unconscious mind in which direction the future lies. Allow your unconscious mind to point in that direction.

If you still haven't revealed your Time line to yourself then don't worry, just as our Time lines themselves are individual, the best way for us to see our Time lines are individual too! A powerful and practical way to reveal your Time line is to 'Walk the Line.' Imagine you do know your Time line and put it on the floor. Which end is your past and which is your future? Place memories along the Time line and walk along it. Because this is a physical exercise, as well as a mental one, there is a chance that you may feel strongly connected to the memories as you walk along with them. You might see yourself in the memory, or you may see the memory through your own eyes. This is an exceptionally useful tool called 'association'—we'll get to how to use that to your advantage soon!

If you still have problems seeing your Time line there could be specific reasons for this. The unconscious mind protects us from harm. There may be a part of you that objects to your seeing your time line. This part may be protecting you from painful memories, or it may be shielding you from worries you have about future events.

Thank that part of yourself for protecting you. Reassure it that you are now competent and old enough to view these memories or fears, in order to deal with and eliminate them. Tell that part of yourself that you are not going to destroy it. Ask this part of yourself what its intent is, what its purpose is. Tell this part of yourself that you want to help it to accomplish this; when you understand this part of yourself, when you feel united in purpose with it, you will get a positive response and with it permission to access your Time line.

Gestalt Psychology and the Time Line:

As was mentioned in the introduction—' A Brief History of the Time Line,' the way in which we store time and the conception of NLP and Time line therapy are closely linked to gestalt therapy, that being the process and interconnection of associated thoughts and memories.

Have you ever had something trigger off a powerful memory? Caught sight of someone who reminded you of someone in your past? Have you ever smelled a smell or heard a sound that takes you back years? This reaction represents a "Gestalt"—a connected collection of memories. What makes a gestalt so influential in what (and how) we remember (and think) is that the memories link back to a **S**ignificant **E**motional **E**xperience (SEE). This is one of the factors that make Time Line Therapy™ so powerful. The link between all of our memories, our experiences, emotions, expectations and aspirations provides us with both foundation and direction. When you know where those memories are, when you know where to best position your future desires, then you have discovered a very powerful tool indeed to help you in life.

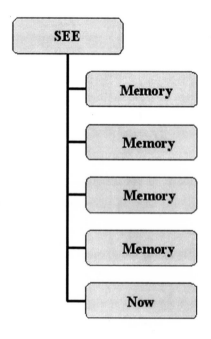

Retrospective use of your Time line:

So now that you know where your Time line lies, and understand how it stores memories and hopes, it's time to begin to experience the magic that is using it, yes? Well the backwards use of the Time technique relies on finding the significant emotional Experience (SEE). By doing this you are, in effect, 'getting to the root of things.' The major benefit in doing this is something that anyone who has ever tried gardening could tell you about—if you don't dig up the roots, the unwanted plant comes back. NLP's experts have rightfully incorporated the work of other academic disciplines into their practice, and when it comes to the backwards use of Time lines then much import has been placed on work such as the sociologist Morris Massey's study of human development.

As mentioned before, though, NLP is primarily interested in processes. So when it comes to the process of going back in time to find a time before SEE's, a time when everything was possible and Gestalts were yet to form, then Matt Hudson recommends going back to the age of two. This provides you with a certain route into the early imprint stage of a brain's development—a wonderful platform to creating new patterns of behaviour and ways of thinking!

Whether you are going back to this early 'default' position, or are actively dealing with a particular SEE, it is the norm to look at the childhood and adolescent development as the route of the gestalt will almost always be found in the 'under twenty' memory category. The 'presenting problem' i.e. the issue that you are having a problem with, is very commonly *not* the root Significant Emotional Experience.

Association/Disassociation:

Association and disassociation are two side of the same coin, and they are one of the easiest and most powerful way to control past memories and future dreams. In short, you are very probably 'associated' right now. You are reading this with your own eyes, you are in your head, aware of how you are feeling right now and looking out at the world through your eyes. Disassociating involves seeing yourself, not being in yourself. It is the use of your experience and intellect to imagine yourself in any hypothetical situation, looking at yourself from the outside (often above).

If you are 'in time' (associated) and lock into a past memory, you will experience that memory as if you are there and it is happening now. You will relive the memory, seeing things through your own eyes, with all the incumbent emotions.

If you are using past good memories to empower yourself and realign yourself on the right track in life, then doing this (associating) is a good thing indeed. It will increase your sense of who you are and where you come from. It will remind you of strengths you had forgotten that you have, and it will evoke the emotions and reasoning behind why you set out on a certain path in life.

Contrarily, if you are impeded in your present and your future because of a SEE in your past, then disassociating from it will allow you to judge that memory, as it was then, more subjectively and, now, looking back on how powerful that event used to be and remembering dispassionately what it was back then in your past, you can know, now, that you have changed that memory from one which you relived to one which can no longer affect you and can be examined where it is, in your past.

Visions of Time:

Each chapter in *The Wizard of Was* demonstrates the power that control over your Time line will bring you. You will learn how to follow the path of the Wizard to the River of Time. You can try it now, or in a little while when you have read these words and thought about them. When you are ready, relax sitting or relax standing up. Imagine yourself floating out of yourself, up, high up above your body so that when you look down you will see your Time line beneath you, flowing from your past, through your present and on into your future. You will experience any number of different emotions now that you are above your Time line you will feel empowered, or enlightened, or liberated or simply good. After all, you have just 'risen above it all.'

Now you have arrived at the beginning of your future and I'm wondering if you've even begun to notice the changes within you, yet? Are you noticing the difference in others and considering that maybe they must have changed because you **can't have changed now, can't you?** That's right! You may want to consider that the more you use your mind as an effective time machine, the more choices you can gain from a magnificent future. Isn't it time now for you to have the perfect past as you realise that everyone who starred in it then did the best that they could at that time, whilst you consider this can you also become aware that as you look back with grace in your heart and soul, you can effortlessly let go of all that is no longer is but is now WAS.